ÁSATRÚ
FOR BEGINNERS

ÁSATRÚ
FOR BEGINNERS

A MODERN HEATHEN'S GUIDE TO THE ANCIENT NORTHERN WAY

MATHIAS NORDVIG, PhD

ROCKRIDGE PRESS

For general information on our other products and services or to obtain technical support, please contact our Customer Care Department within the United States at (866) 744-2665, or outside the United States at (510) 253-0500.

Rockridge Press publishes its books in a variety of electronic and print formats. Some content that appears in print may not be available in electronic books, and vice versa.

Interior and Cover Designer: Patricia Fabricant
Art Producer: Tom Hood
Editor: Sean Newcott
Production Editor: Ruth Sakata Corley
Illustrations © Shutterstock, 2020; Author photograph courtesy of Erica Lindberg

ISBN: Print 978-1-64739-763-0 | eBook 978-1-64739-764-7
R1

TO MY MOTHER, ELSE–JULIE NORDVIG.
A STRONG HEATHEN WOMAN.

CONTENTS

WELCOME TO ÁSATRÚ

Defined by the belief in the ancient Norse gods, Ásatrú is also referred to as *heathenry* and its practitioners are called *heathens*. Ásatrú is a modern neo-pagan belief that has its foundation in the pre-Christian religions of Scandinavia and Northern Europe. Although the Nordic countries converted to Christianity some 1,000 years ago, many of the old ideas, beliefs, and myths about the Norse gods lived on. They were written down in Iceland and elsewhere in Scandinavia in the medieval period, from about 1100 to 1500 CE. Modern Ásatrú was coined as a belief and way of life in the 19th century, but only became well-known and practiced in Europe and North America in the 1970s. Since then, Ásatrú has become a popular modern spirituality with established communities across the world, especially in Europe and North America. In the Scandinavian countries, Ásatrú has become the fastest growing spirituality. In Iceland, Ásatrú is the country's largest non-Christian belief community, with some 3,000 registered heathens of the country's 320,000 people. In the United States of America, the number of heathens is difficult to capture and count, but I estimate that it is in the tens of thousands. There are many reasons that it is hard to reach an accurate number. One reason is that many heathens do not organize in large, open groups. They tend to gather in smaller groups, with family or friends. One thing is for sure, though: today, Ásatrú is practiced and celebrated all over the world!

As a Danish national and scholar of Norse mythology, I too am a heathen. In fact, I was raised by heathen parents. Born in Denmark, I spent a good part of my childhood in Greenland, but I have also lived in Iceland, and frequently visited Norway and Sweden throughout my life. Over the years, I've met personal friends from heathen communities all over the world, from Argentina in the south to Canada in the north, from New Zealand in the east to California in the west. I have partaken in rituals with heathens in the rolling Danish hills, the Swedish forests, the Norwegian fjords, the Bavarian Alps, the windblown shores of Iceland, the plains of the American Midwest, and, especially, the Rocky Mountains, where I have lived for many years now. Growing up with Norse mythology as a fundamental part of my Scandinavian culture and a part of my family's spirituality, it was natural for me to study it in college. Since I finished my PhD on Norse mythology in 2014, I have proudly taught at the university level on the Vikings, Norse mythology, and other Scandinavian subjects.

With *Ásatrú for Beginners*, I look forward to sharing nearly 40 years of heathen experience with you. My hope is that this book will serve as an illuminating and empowering introduction for you, if you believe in—or are interested in—in the Norse gods. In the chapters that follow, you will encounter a solid history of Ásatrú and the pre-Christian religions of Scandinavia. You will learn about how the modern heathen movements came into existence and what this modern spirituality is all about. Ásatrú is a free spirituality without dogma, and this guide is just one perspective on what heathens believe. Throughout this book, I have done my best to represent the global heathen community as accurately as possible, while adding my own personal knowledge, based on my many years as a heathen and a professional scholar. With this in mind, I invite you on a journey to learn more about the ancient ways of heathenism.

CHAPTER ONE

WHAT IS ÁSATRÚ?

Ásatrú is a modern spirituality based in the traditions, folklore, and mythology of Northern Europe and particularly Scandinavia. Around 1,000 years ago, Scandinavians and other peoples in Northern Europe converted to Christianity but, for many, the gods and spirits of the old pre-Christian religions were still important. People continued to tell stories about them and, in some ways, continued to venerate them. Eventually, some of the stories about the ancient gods and spirits were written down by historians and antiquarians, who were interested in preserving knowledge about the past. These texts have since been used in modern times to revive a spirituality centered around the Norse gods.

UNDERSTANDING ÁSATRÚ

Ásatrú is a modern Icelandic word that was originally used by Danish scholars in the 19th century when referring to the pre-Christian religion in Scandinavia. In its Danish and Swedish forms, it is spelled *asatro*, and in Norwegian, it is spelled *åsatru*. The Scandinavians all pronounce the word differently, but in English, the Icelandic way of saying it would phonetically sound like *ow-sa-troo*. The word is a combination of the Norse word *áss* (god, spirit. Plural: *æsir*) and the word *trú* (belief). Ásatrú means *belief in the æsir*, and people who believe in the æsir can be referred to as Ásatrúar, with the Icelandic plural suffix *–ar* at the end of the word. The word came into use in the English language, especially in the United States, in the 1970s, under influence from Iceland. In modern English, most heathens use it in the sense "belief in the æsir," but some also emphasize *trust* in the æsir.

Ásatrú, Heathen, or Pagan?

There's an old Scandinavian saying: *A beloved child has many names!* This is certainly true in the case of modern Norse-based spirituality. Ásatrú is just one way that people who believe in the Norse gods refer to themselves. Some groups shy away from the word Ásatrú itself and call themselves *heathen* instead. Even in modern English, the word heathen is not often associated with positive connotations. In the medieval period, the word was used to describe people who did not believe in the Christian god and to identify heretics who did not believe in the Christian god in the same way as the established churches. The traditionally Christian way of employing the word heathen comes from another word that is still used in modern English: *pagan*. The word has its origin in the Latin word *pagus* (village), which the early Christians in Rome used to refer to those who had not yet converted; to god-fearing Christians, pagan meant "hillbilly," "redneck," or "backwards." When Christianity moved north and interacted with the Germanic-speaking peoples in Northern Europe, the Latin word was quickly translated into the Germanic languages, and Christians in Northern Europe began referring to non-Christians as heathens.

Originally, the word heathen meant *a person of the commons*. The commons were the part of a local tribal territory that everyone could use if they needed to. This suggests that when pre-Christian Germanic peoples called someone "heathen," it meant that they followed the customs and traditions of the community. With the emergence of Christianity, it changed to mean "outsider" and "non-believer." Today, many who believe in the Norse gods call themselves heathens. In some ways, it is because they want to demonstrate to others that they do not believe in the Christian god, and in other ways, it is because many of them have reclaimed the old meaning and want to demonstrate that they believe in community. Heathens practice *heathenry* or *heathenism*: the old way, the traditional customs. To them, it is a positive word, and they share many commonalities in terms of beliefs and rituals with other neo-pagan groups, such as Wiccans and witches.

The Different Ways of Being Heathen

When it comes to Ásatrú, there are many ways that one can be heathen. Some put strong focus on the æsir, others on the vanir, and yet others are most focused on ancestors and the spirits of the land. In Ásatrú, both in North America and Europe, there is often a tendency to focus on regions and countries of origin in Europe. Many Americans come to Ásatrú and heathenry because they have some ancestry from Northern Europe. Naturally, they take an interest in forging their heathen path with reference to where their ancestors are from. For instance, if someone has Norwegian ancestors and decides to practice heathenry, they often will be interested in how the spirituality was specifically practiced in Norway during ancient times. Yet there are also many who become Ásatrúar and heathens without having any ancestral ties to Scandinavia and Northern Europe, instead fashioning their beliefs in a more general sense, using the history, traditions, and literatures from the entire region as a backdrop for their beliefs. As a Scandinavian heathen, I am greatly honored to see that there are people of all races and ethnicities who find our customs and traditions valuable, and I welcome everyone to Ásatrú, regardless of their origin.

In Europe, there are many different groups identifying as Ásatrú and heathens who specifically worship the Norse gods. You can find many such groups in Iceland and Scandinavia, the United Kingdom, Germany, the Netherlands, and Austria, but there are also several in France, Spain, Italy, Poland, Finland and the Baltic countries, and even Russia. Each group has their own unique way of being heathen. Often, they identify with the history and tradition of Germanic peoples in their country and region. In Iceland, there is a well-known national group called *Ásatrúarfélagið* (The Ásatrúar Community), and in Norway, there are the two organizations known as *Forn Sed* (Ancient Custom) and *Åsatrufelleskapet Bifrost* (The Ásatrú-community Bifrost). In Sweden, there is *Samfundet Forn Sed Sverige* (The Community Ancient Custom Sweden) and *Samfälligheten för Nordisk Sed* (The Community for Nordic Customs), and in Denmark, there is *Forn Siðr* (Ancient Custom) and *Asatrofællesskabet i Danmark* (The Ásatrúar Community of Denmark). One thing you may notice is that several of the groups use the term "forn sed" or "forn siðr" which means "ancient custom." This is also a common way of referring to being heathen or Ásatrúar in Scandinavia.

In the UK and in North America, there are groups that identify as Anglo-Saxon heathens rather than Ásatrú. These groups are more focused on the pre-Christian past of the Germanic tribes—the Angles, Saxons, and Jutes—who founded Anglo-Saxon England. In the Netherlands and in North America, there are also groups that identify with the Frisians, an ethnic minority that still lives along the coast that stretches from the Netherlands to Denmark. In Germany, there are many groups that identify with local tribes and peoples that historically have been present in a particular region there. This is also the case, to an extent, in Belgium and France. In France, Spain, and Italy, some groups identify with the Germanic peoples who migrated into those areas some 1,500 years ago: the Franks, Salians, Burgundians, Alemans, Goths, and Langobards.

A Religion or Spirituality?

You may have noticed by now that it is not easy to say that Ásatrúar and heathens just represent one group, belief, or way of seeing the world. There are many different groups that define what it means to be heathen in their own way. The same is true for whether you use the word *religion* to define and understand Ásatrú. For the purposes of this book, I have decided to use the word "spirituality" rather than "religion." The word religion often carries the sense of a church, with a priesthood and dogma, and that is not at all what heathenry is. Heathenry is a non-dogmatic community belief, which means there is no scripture that a member or believer must follow and there are no clergy and priests who hold authority. Every group has their own way—their own rules and their own leaders. Ásatrúarfélagið in Iceland has a board of directors and an *allsherjargoði*, a spiritual leader. *Allsherjargoði* means "All regions' priest." If it is masculine, the word for priest is spelled *goði*, and when it is feminine, the word is spelled *gyðja*. There are also local *goðar* and *gyðjur* in Iceland, who are in charge of leading rituals. The word is also used in the other Scandinavian countries, where it is typically spelled *gode/goder* and *gydje/gydjer*.

Since the Icelandic Ásatrú community was founded in 1972, they have had four allsherjargoðar: the founder, Sveinbjörn Beinteinsson, who served until his death in December 1993; Jörmundur Ingi, who served until 2002, when he was relieved of duty by the board of directors; Jónína Kristín Berg was interim allsherjargyðja after him; and Hilmar Örn Hilmarsson was elected in 2003 and has been in charge since. In other countries, the structures are notably different. In Denmark and Norway, the Ásatrú organizations pride themselves on strong democratic structures. Åsatrufel-lesskapet Bifrost in Norway, for instance, elects all members of office and has no supreme spiritual leader. In Denmark, the organization Forn Siðr has an elected board with a president, but each year they also elect a *þulr*, a spiritual leader who only serves a one-year term. In Forn Siðr, however, any member can be a gode or gydje and perform ceremonies such as weddings by obtaining a time-limited permit.

In the United States, the major organization, The Troth, has a High Rede, or a high council, consisting of elected members. The organization also has stewards who represent the organization locally, from Hawaii to as far away as Germany. The group additionally has elders, who attained their honorific title through a minimum of a decade of service and who enjoy some respect as a clergy.

As you can see, there are many variations in how Ásatrúar and hea-thens decide to congregate and practice their beliefs in an organized way.

Ásatrúar and heathens believe in the Norse gods in many different ways, and they do not always agree on how you should practice these beliefs. Ásatrú is first and foremost a personal spirituality that Ásatrúar formulate themselves. Many practitioners are solitary or only practice in a tight-knit group of family and friends. They do not necessarily think that they need an organization or the trappings of an established religion to practice their beliefs.

What brings all these groups together? At a very basic level, they are united by the importance of the Germanic and Norse gods. But the way that people believe in the Germanic-Norse gods differs widely. In North America and some places in Europe, people who identify as Ásatrú and heathen often believe in the existence of the Germanic-Norse gods in the same way that Christians and Muslims believe in their gods. However, in Scandinavia, and particularly in Iceland, the number of people who would say that they definitively believe in the Germanic-Norse gods is very low. In a 2006–7 study of Ásatrú in Iceland, only 2 percent of those surveyed said they believed in the gods. While there are certainly people who believe in the gods in Scandinavia, it is important to understand that *belief* is not the most important part of being Ásatrú and heathen.

This may be difficult to comprehend because you are likely accustomed to the idea that belief is an important part of being religious or of having spirituality. For Ásatrúar and heathens, belief is less important than how you live your life. Many would say the idea that belief is central belongs to Abrahamic religions, but not as much to the heathen spiritualities. Your actions count more than your words and your thoughts, and for many Ásatrúar and heathens, it is more important that you do what is best for your family, your community, and yourself, than it is to believe a certain way.

THE ORIGIN OF ÁSATRÚ

Long before Abrahamic religions, people across Europe, Asia, and the entire world believed in many different gods. The belief in many gods is called *polytheism* (and sometimes also *animism*). When we reference polytheism we're often referring to beliefs like the ancient Greek and Roman religions, whereas animism is often used to describe religions that are less organized and more tribal, in the sense that they did not unfold in urban settings. There are other differences between polytheism and animism, but that is the most important one. To better understand Ásatrú in the 21st century, I will have to take you on a historical journey of religion in Europe.

The Stone Age

In the Mesolithic Period, the part of the Stone Age before the introduction of farming in Europe, religion was focused on hunting practices; for instance, shamans would perform rituals to provide a generous hunt. Rituals and beliefs were centered around the important components of subsisting: gathering food, birth, illness, being initiated into a role in life, forming personal partnerships, and, of course, death. The beliefs and rituals did not disappear in the Neolithic period, when farming was introduced in Europe, but they probably became more complex as society also became more complex.

Around 8,000 years ago, the first evidence of farming appeared in Southern Europe. Farming spread from Anatolia in modern-day Turkey, through Greece and the Balkans, to the Italian peninsula and northward. With farming, new rituals were introduced. People began to sacrifice animals and offer portions of their food and drink to gods that were in control of the fertility of the fields, crops, and harvest. Society became more complex as people gathered in urban centers. With urbanism came new forms of government—city states—and new life roles that people could take on. In spite of this, many aspects of the older hunter-gatherer lifestyle persisted; they were not simply abandoned as civilization evolved.

Farming was introduced to Northern Europe between 6,000 and 4,000 years ago, depending on the region. This was the period when Scandinavians learned how to farm, and this would also be the time when their religion developed with a similar level of complexity as in the southern parts of Europe, but without the urban centers. During this period, at least parts of the religion that would later be the religion of the Vikings (for instance) came into existence. What is not solidly grasped is what form it took, how it was practiced, and what beliefs people held. One of the most evident developments during the period was that burial mounds became widely used as community graves. The tradition of burying either one or more people in burial mounds persisted in Scandinavia until its people converted to Christianity about 1,000 years ago.

The Bronze Age

The Bronze Age came to Northern Europe and Scandinavia around 1700 to 500 BCE. The introduction of bronze as a new material to make tools and weapons changed the ways people conducted trade, built structures, and practiced religion. In Scandinavian archaeological remains from this period, we see ceremonial axes, swords, helmets with horns, and the procession horns called *lures*. During the same time, Scandinavians made rock carvings. The rock carvings feature scenes of people hunting, plowing fields, sailing, and performing rituals. What especially stands out in the rock carvings are the depictions of people rowing canoe-like boats, as well as a large figure that holds a hammer or axe in front of him. This figure is depicted in multiple carvings, and it looks very similar to Thor, the thunder god. A new feature of burials also appears: stone ship-settings. It is clear that during this period in Scandinavia, a tribal warrior society became more dominant and maritime pursuits became an important part of life.

Religion in the Bronze Age both developed with society and lived side by side with ancient elements that had been part of life since the hunter cultures of the Stone Age. Gods and spirits in control of the fields and farming became part of religious life when farming was introduced, but when metal arrived in Scandinavia and Northern Europe, new and more complex aspects of society developed. Specifically, it appears as though trade and territory developed a greater importance. It is possible that chieftains rose to power, too, though they shared power with a tribal council or assembly. Still, such chieftains almost certainly would have had new ideas of rulership and gods attached to them. The Bronze Age was also a time when Northern Europe saw greater integration with Southern Europe and a time that saw trade flourish. Ideas, gods, and spiritual concepts would certainly have migrated from south to north and influenced the way that Scandinavians saw their religions.

The Celtic Iron Age

In Scandinavia, the Iron Age began around 500 BCE. The Iron Age saw the first evidence of the Germanic cultures in Northern Europe. Celtic cultures had been spreading across central Europe for some time, and their religious imprint on Scandinavian culture is unmistakable. The Gundestrup cauldron from northern Jutland in Denmark is a distinct Celtic artifact, depicting deities like the horned Cernunnos, the thunder-god Taranis, and perhaps even Morgana, known from the Gallic religion in France before the Roman invasions. Roman historians report being harassed by invading tribes from the north, such as the Cimbri, Ambrones, and Teutones, during the period 105 to 101 BCE. (In later geographic descriptions, the Jutland Peninsula is referred to as the Cimbrian Peninsula.) Geographers and historians from the Roman empire seem to agree that the Cimbri originated from the southern Scandinavian region. The tribal name of the Teutones is linguistically similar to the Proto-Germanic word *þeudō, which meant *people*. This suggests that at least the Cimbri and Teutones may have been Germanic-speaking peoples, and their appearance in Roman literature in the last decade of the second century BCE is the first evidence of Germanic tribes in European history. Roman historians record that the people of the time sacrificed both humans and animals, which compares well with archaeological evidence of similar practices in Scandinavia during the same period of time.

The Roman Iron Age

The Germanic peoples appear in Roman literature again in Julius Caesar's *Commentaries on the Gallic Wars* from the middle of the first century CE, but they emerge fully with the Roman writer Tacitus's ethnographic work *Germania* from circa 98 CE. The Romans referred to the land north of the Rhine as *Germania*, which is how the people from the region came to be known as *Germanics* or *Germans*. Tacitus described many interesting aspects of Northern European and Scandinavian religion. He mentioned that Germanic peoples had female leaders who could perform witchcraft. He described specific gods that the Germanic peoples worshipped, but he gave them

Latin names. He particularly talked about Mercury (Óðinn) and Hercules/Jupiter (Þórr). Tacitus also described a procession ritual with a wagon that carried a goddess named Nerthus around in the countryside on an island in the Northern Sea. Nerthus is etymologically the same name as Njörðr, the god of seafaring in Norse mythology (the island in question could be one of the Danish islands). Around the same time that Tacitus wrote his account, people sacrificed several wagons in waterbodies in the Danish area. Tacitus also mentioned that they sacrificed humans in the lakes in Germania. There are several finds of sacrificed humans in the northern German area and the Danish area from the period 0 to 600 CE. The "bog-bodies" are well-preserved human bodies, where skin, hair, and teeth have been preserved by the oxygen-free environment in the sludge found at the bottom of ancient lakes.

The Migration Age

Runic inscriptions begin appearing circa 150 CE. While runes are simply a letter system like the alphabet, it is obvious that they were used in magical practices from the beginning. Warriors, religious authorities, chieftains, and kings were the ones who knew runes; in the beginning, runes were not for the common people.

In the first 500 years CE, Germanic peoples migrated from northern Germany, Scandinavia, and the coastal regions of modern-day Poland. They traveled as far as Ukraine in the east, Greece and Bulgaria in the southeast, Spain and North Africa in the south, and the British Isles in the west. The Goths established kingdoms in Italy, France, and Spain. The Anglo-Saxons migrated to Britain and founded England. The Franks founded what would later become France. Traces of the precursor to the Viking Age religion are found in the cultures of the early migrating Germanic peoples, whose histories were written down in Latin in Late Antiquity. For instance, the Langobards (Long-beards) are said to have received their tribal name from Óðinn or Wōðan.

The Goths feature prominently in both runic inscriptions and in later medieval Nordic literature in Scandinavia. Both the Goths and the Heruli claimed origin in "Thule," the Greco-Roman name for Scandinavia. When the Langobards destroyed the Herulian kingdom in what is now Austria and Hungary in the period around 495 to 508 CE, the remaining Heruli appear to have migrated back to Scandinavia.

During the same period, around 500 CE, runic inscriptions with the name or title "Erilaz" appear in Scandinavia. The inscription is believed to be the Germanic version of the Latinized tribal name "Heruli." Eventually, "Erilaz" evolved to an honorific title in Scandinavia and became the basis for the title *earl* in English and *jarl* in Scandinavian.

During the Migration Period, from circa 200 CE to 600 CE, Scandinavian contact with Rome intensified. Germanic peoples in Scandinavia learned many things from the Romans, and their contact had a direct impact on how they practiced their religion. Drinking rituals became important in Scandinavia under direct influence from the Roman *Bacchanalia*, the orgies dedicated to the god Bacchus. The Scandinavians seem to have venerated Óðinn in the role of Bacchus in their rituals. The Rhineland area was the hotspot for cultural exchange. During the period 0 to 300 CE in the Rhineland, Celtic, Germanic, and Roman peoples interacted and exchanged ideas—and gods. The cult of the *matronae* became an important religious practice in the area; the *matronae* consisted of three female deities who rule over fate, life, death, and fertility. Farther north in Scandinavia, the *matronae* became the *nornir, fylgjur, dísir,* and *valkyrjur:* female guardian spirits who rule over fate, luck, family, the newly born, and death. It is obvious that the Germanic peoples mixed aspects of Roman religion with their own due to various inscriptions from Frisia in the Netherlands, and from England, where votive stones are dedicated to Mars *þingsus* and Mars *halamarðus.* Mars is the Roman god of war, but the title *þingsus* is a Latinized version of the Germanic word for "assembly," while *halamarðus* is a Germanic word meaning "murderer of men." The inscriptions were likely made by Germanic warriors present within the Roman armies.

Beginning around 300 CE, the Germanic tribes in south-central Europe began to convert to Christianity. Some likely converted before then, but the big push in which Christian Germanic empires were created occurred during that period. In the late 400s CE, the Franks created the Frankish Empire, which ultimately displaced Rome as the foremost military power in Western Europe. They converted to Christianity in the early 500s, and from the last half of the 500s CE, the Franks sent missionaries to Britain to convert the Anglo-Saxons. The last heathen king in England was Penda of Mercia, who fell in 655 CE. As Christianity spread in central-western Europe, the religion of the Germanic peoples farther to the north also changed. Local kings and chieftains in Scandinavia began building central sites. The central sites were typically comprised of temple complexes with a central hall, a temple building, and other features such as marketplaces and blacksmiths. In the central sites, seasonal rituals would also likely have taken place. The people of the region were required to participate in the rituals and pay taxes to the temples. The king or chieftain who ruled at the time would have had a band of warriors called a hirð living with him at all times. That is likely the origin of the cult of Óðinn as a war-god and as god of kings.

During the Vendel period, circa 500 to 700 CE, images of Óðinn's wolf- and bear-warriors appear on armory and other artifacts in Scandinavia. The adornments are most certainly connected to the mythical *úlfheðnar* and *berserkir* that are described in Norse mythology. From Sweden to East Anglia, imagery of the same warrior cult dedicated to Óðinn appear in this period. During the same time, the Old English poem *Beowulf* was composed—originally a heathen poem honoring ancient Scandinavian heroes and kings in the setting of a hall similar to the central sites. The English historian Bede (672 to 735 CE) also mentions that the English used to worship a goddess named Ēostre, undoubtedly a fertility goddess similar to the *matronae* on the continent and Nerthus in Scandinavia.

The Viking Age

Charlemagne became king of the Franks in 768 CE. In the years that followed, he began expanding his empire, and in 772 CE, he invaded the still heathen kingdom of Saxony in northern Germany under the pretense of converting the Saxons to Christianity. Charlemagne first invaded Engria and destroyed the holy symbol *Îrminsûl*, a pillar representing the world tree, known from Norse mythology as *Yggdrasill*. He ousted the Saxon king Widukind, who went to exile in Denmark and later returned with mercenaries to fight off the invaders. In 782 CE, Charlemagne executed

4,500 heathen Saxons at the Blood Court in Verden. The battle for Saxony waged back and forth until 804 CE, when Charlemagne was finally victorious. From then on, Christianity moved northward and into Scandinavia. During the same time, non-Christian Scandinavians made incursions into the British Isles and began conducting raids (as "Vikings") along the northwestern coasts of Europe.

It is typical to set the beginning of the Viking Age to 793 CE, when Scandinavian raiders reportedly sacked Saint Cuthbert's monastery on the northern English island Lindisfarne. However, the Viking Age probably began a century before that with naval trade between Scandinavia and Western Europe. The important trade port of Ripa in southern Denmark was already in existence in 700 CE, trading goods with Frisia to the south and Norway to the north. As such, it was one of the hotspots for cultural exchange between Scandinavians, Frisians, Anglo-Saxons, Franks, and German Saxons. It is probably through Ripa that Scandinavians became familiar with the stories about the ancient Frisian hero Wayland, called Vølundr in Norse, and the Burgundian hero Siegfried (Sîvrit), known as Sigurðr Fáfnisbani in Norse. Siegfried is the hero of the *Song of the Nibelungs* and probably the most popular hero in pre-modern Northern Europe. Versions of his story are found across Scandinavia: on the largest known runic inscription, the Ramsund stone; in woodcarvings on the Hyllestad stave church in Norway; in Danish and Faroese ballads; in medieval Eddic poems; in Snorri Sturluson's *Edda*; and in *Vølsunga saga*, the medieval saga about Sigurðr that was written in 13th century Iceland.

The extent to which Viking Age religion in Scandinavia looked like what Norse literature and other historical sources describe is uncertain. We know that Scandinavians in the Viking Age had temples where they sacrificed to the gods Óðinn, Þórr, and Freyr, as it is described by Adam of Bremen in *History of the Archbishopric of Hamburg-Bremen*. In it, he details a feast that takes place in Uppsala in Sweden every ninth year, where 72 animals and humans would be hung as sacrifices in the trees in a sacred grove. Some would also be drowned in a well. Thietmar of Merseburg describes a similar ritual that took place in Denmark in Hleiþra (Lejre), where 99 animals and humans would be sacrificed. Dudo of St. Quentin, in his *History of the Normans*, writes that the Viking ancestors of the Normans would make sacrifices before embarking on naval journeys.

The most remarkable descriptions of Viking Age religion come from the Muslim emissaries Ahmad Ibn Fadlan and Yaqub Al-Tartushi. Al-Tartushi visited Haiþabú (Hedeby) in southern Denmark and described how Scandinavians would make sacrifices of animals and share the meat with their community. According to him, they worshipped the North Star and likely regarded the omens of stars in a similar way that people now look to astrology. They would also sing songs that Al-Tartushi described as sounding like barking dogs, and they would wear eye makeup. Women also had the right to divorce their husbands. Ibn Fadlan encountered the Viking Rus, founders of the medieval Russian empire, on an expedition on the Volga river in Russia in 921 CE. He described their traditions in great detail. He wrote that the men carried swords, knives, and axes at all times; that they were tattooed from neck to toe; and that the women were adorned with bead necklaces hanging on their chests. When a merchant Rus was going to the market to sell his goods, Ibn Fadlan writes that he would go to a grove and offer bread, onion, beer, milk, and honey to wooden posts with carved faces representing the gods. The man would lie down in front of them and pray. If he had good luck, he would return and sacrifice animals. Parts of the animals would be given to the gods; other parts would be given as charity.

Ibn Fadlan does not name the gods that received the offerings, but from Scandinavian place-names, there is evidence that many of the gods mentioned in later Norse literature were venerated in the Viking Age. There are ancient place-names scattered in the Nordic landscapes dedicated to Þórr, Óðinn, Njörðr (male), Freyr, Ullr, Týr, Frigg, Freyja, Niærþer (female Njörðr), all of whom are known from Norse literature. However, there are also names of deities in the place-names that are not identified in any literature. A deity named Hærn appears in place-names in Norway, and the name or title Lytir appears in Sweden. Aside from that, the way the place-names dedicated to deities are spread out indicates that there was much diversity in the worship of gods in pre-Christian Scandinavia. Based on place-names, Ullr was a very popular god in central Norway and Sweden, but nonexistent in Denmark. Týr, on the other hand, only has places dedicated to him in Denmark, except for one on an island off the

Norwegian coast. Iceland has no place-names dedicated to any of the Norse gods but, in turn, has several sites that are called *hof*, which means *temple*.

Aside from place-names and various accounts from outside observers, we also have some homegrown sources from the Viking Age from Scandinavia. Archaeological finds from the Viking Age can help us understand what Scandinavians believed in. The many runestones that were carved and placed in the landscape attest to religious ideas in different ways. Some invoke gods or carry magical inscriptions and others have imagery that can be linked directly to the written mythology. From archaeological finds, we also have statuettes and artifacts that are clearly religious. A popular item from the Viking Age was a Thor's hammer pendant, which was worn by people to demonstrate their belief in the gods. In other cases, we have depictions of gods and mythical beings, such as the face of Loki on a stone from a Danish Viking Age smithy, and Óðinn on his eight-legged horse Sleipnir on the Ardre picture-stones from Viking Age Sweden. The figures are readily identifiable because they were described in Norse literature, written in Iceland in the 1200s. The main sources are Snorri Sturluson's *Edda*, Eddic and skaldic poetry, and the saga literature.

Norse Literature

The most accessible, but also least trustworthy, source material on the Norse gods is medieval literature from the period 1100 to 1500 CE, originating from Iceland, Norway, and Denmark. During the period, Icelanders wrote *sagas*, a semi-historical genre of literature based in oral tales that existed in the time before literature was introduced in Scandinavia. Some stories were also written in Norway and in Denmark. In Denmark, the historian Saxo (circa 1160 to 1209) used Norse mythology as a main source to the first nine books in his Latin compilation on Danish history, *The Deeds of the Danes*. The main theme of the Icelandic sagas and Saxo's Danish history is the Viking Age and the time preceding it. They give details and descriptions of pre-Christian beliefs and ideas, rituals, gods, and other spirits. The literature is highly useful to understanding what the pre-Christian Nordic religion was, but it is also important to know that it was written by Christians, several centuries after the conversion to Christianity took place. It may therefore not accurately reflect the beliefs of pre-Christian Scandinavians, but it is important to modern heathens, because it offers a glimpse of what life may have been like during ancient times.

Another important genre of literature is traditional Nordic poetry, of which there are two types: Skaldic and Eddic poetry. Eddic poetry is a traditional Germanic type of poetry that has its roots in 300 to 400 CE, during the Migration Age. The primary collection of Eddic poems is the manuscript *Codex Regius of the Poetic Edda* from 1270 CE. It contains 10 poems about the Norse gods and another 29 about ancient heroes like Sigurðr Fáfnisbani. The collection was written in Iceland or Norway and seems to have been used for drama and performance. There are several types of poetic meter in Eddic poetry, and at least two of them, Fornyrðislag (Meter of Ancient Words) and Ljóðaháttr (Meter of Songs), are closely related to the meter in *Beowulf* and the old German *Hildebrandslied*. Eddic poetry was a common Germanic form of poetry that was used in ritual and the performance of myths and stories of ancient heroes. For modern heathens, Eddic poetry has become very important in *blót* and other rituals because it is popular and engaging when incorporated within a performance.

Skaldic poetry was invented in Scandinavia during the 700s CE as a form of praise poetry, where skalds (poets) would compose poems about kings and great warriors. The poetry is very complex and makes use of metaphors and analogies, called *heiti* and *kenningar*, which are based in Norse mythology. Where the composers of Eddic poems are unknown, most skaldic poems have known composers, who can be located in time and place. In the Viking Age, all Scandinavian kings—even English, Scottish, and Irish kings—would have skalds at their court. Most of the skalds originated from Iceland, where the poetic tradition became an important tool for social advancement. Icelanders would travel to Scandinavia and the British Isles and make a living by becoming popular poets. For this reason, most of the sources on Norse mythology have been written in medieval Iceland.

An Icelandic chieftain Snorri Sturluson (1179 to 1241 CE) is likely the most important author of Norse mythology. In 1220 CE, he wrote *Edda*, the most comprehensive description of Norse mythology. Written in four parts,

Edda was intended to give young Icelandic poets guidance in the ancient art of skaldic poetry.

The first part of *Edda* is a prologue where Snorri gives a Christian explanation for why people were pagan. In Snorri's mind, the world was created by the Christian god and was intended to be Christian from the beginning. He therefore had to explain that it was because people forgot the name of the Christian god and began worshipping successful humans instead. The people were, according to him, the æsir who came from Asia. It is not a coincidence that Snorri says they came from Asia: He wanted to portray the paganism in Scandinavia as an immigrant, outsider religion that had nothing to do with the "true faith."

The second part of *Edda* is called *Gylfaginning*, the "Delusion of Gylfi." The chapter sets the stage for how people in Scandinavia were tricked by the æsir who migrated there from Troy. Gylfi, a king in Sweden, travels to visit the æsir and to ask them questions about their belief. They tell him the stories of Norse mythology, and at the end of the chapter, Snorri writes that people began believing because the æsir said the stories had taken place in Scandinavia.

The third part of *Edda* is called *Skáldskaparmál*, the "Language of Poetry," and it has a similar setting as *Gylfaginning*. Set in a time after Gylfi questioned the æsir, the chapter takes place at a banquet where the æsir are visiting Gymir. At a dinner conversation at the banquet, Bragi explains skaldic poetry to Gymir and includes many myths in his explanations.

The final part of *Edda* is the poem *Háttatal*, which gives examples of all the poetic forms in skaldic poetry. Throughout his work, Snorri made use of Eddic and skaldic poetry, as well as folktales and myths in prose, which he knew from sources that are no longer identifiable. While Snorri was a knowledgeable scholar on pre-Christian Scandinavian religion, it is important to remember that he was a Christian, who distorted parts of the mythology and did not in any way condone paganism. He was not a secret heathen! However, Snorri's *Edda* is one of the most accessible sources that modern heathens have of their ancient stories.

THE REBIRTH OF AN ANCIENT RELIGION

In the 1500s, Scandinavian scholars were busy reading the Icelandic saga literature. Snorri's *Edda* was known at universities and colleges and was being studied by theologians. In 1643, the bishop at Iceland's bishopric in Skálholt, Brynjólfr Sveinsson, rediscovered the manuscript containing the Eddic poems. He thought that it was originally written by the first Icelandic historian Sæmundr inn fróði (1056 to 1133 CE), and he recognized that the content was similar to Snorri's *Edda*. For that reason, he called it *Sæmundr's Edda*. It was later discovered that Sæmundr could not have written the collection of poems, since the manuscript was from 1270 CE, long after Sæmundr's death. Nonetheless, Brynjólfr sent the manuscript to his king in Denmark, thus beginning the popularization of Norse mythology.

In the period between 1500 and 1800, Danish and Swedish scholars wrote long investigations of Norse mythology, the Viking Age, and the importance of Odinic warriors in ancient times, mostly to boost national morale in the rivalries between the two countries. Meanwhile, interest in Norse mythology grew in Germany and England for other reasons. For the Germans, the interest began as scholars were searching for the "folk soul" of the Germans, or the 18th century idea that a culture is unified by a deep-seated essence that sits in the core of every person who belongs to it. In England and Scotland, on the other hand, Norse mythology became interesting in the Gothic literature of authors like William Blake and Thomas Gray. They sprinkled their literature with barbaric, pagan Vikings.

Neo-paganism first emerged in the 19th century, although there are traces of some neo-pagan tendencies in Iceland in the 18th century. After several centuries of using Norse mythology as a component in creating the Scandinavian and Germanic identities, knowledge of the Norse gods became commonplace in the populations of Germany, the Netherlands, Austria, Denmark, Norway, Sweden, and Iceland. By the last half of the 19th century, practically every Germanic-speaking country had societies and groups dedicated to the Norse gods, typically Óðinn. Gatherings and rituals took place in the early 20th century as the groups materialized into more formal organizations. However, darkness fell over many of them as they became more and more involved with the racist German *Völkisch* movement. The old idea that people carried a folk soul was married to the idea of the superior white race, and many saw the ancient Germanic heathens as those who had the pure folk soul. Several of the *Völkisch* heathen movements were directly involved with the Nazi party in Germany during the 1920s and 1930s, but when Hitler took power, he eventually outlawed them and sent some of them to concentration camps. The *Völkisch* ideas lived on after the Second World War in groups calling themselves Odinists or Folkish Ásatrú. "Folkish" is the English translation of *Völkisch*, essentially meaning "white separatist" today.

The 1970s became the true era of the rebirth of Ásatrú: the period of New Age movements, Western fascination with Eastern religions, witchcraft, and Satanism. A particular branch of modern witchcraft called Wicca gained importance in the 1950s. The ideas of Wicca had direct impact on how Ásatrúar envisioned spirituality. The principal idea in Wicca is that gods and goddesses are manifestations of the primal god and goddess. From the beginning of Wicca in the 1930s, Germanic gods had been part of its practice. In the 1970s, Raymond Buckland founded Seax Wica, a particular Saxon-Nordic branch of Wicca. During the 1970s, 1980s, and mid-1990s, Ásatrú and Wicca grew along parallel trajectories. It is not an understatement to say that most rituals that Ásatrúar performed during that period, and still perform today, were either direct borrowings from or strongly influenced by Wicca.

In the middle of the 1990s, many Ásatrúar became conscious of the influence from Wicca and decided to return to the old sources to determine how to create rituals and beliefs that were more in tune with how ancient Nordic-Germanic pagans practiced their religion. Doing so led to the emergence of reconstructionist Ásatrú, where Ásatrúar tried as best as they could to copy beliefs, ideas, and rituals from the Icelandic saga literature. Reconstructionism was initially promoted by one of the original founders of Ásatrú in the United States, Bill Linzie, who had envisioned a modern spirituality that closely adapted what ancient literature described about the pre-Christian Scandinavian religion. However, reconstructionism quickly took an unfortunate direction toward fundamentalist ideas of applying ancient ideas one-to-one to the modern spirituality. Like so many other modern spiritualities, modern Ásatrúar are divided into hardliners and more relaxed practitioners.

The typical modern Ásatrúar is an individual living in an urban environment in North America or Europe. They usually have a steady job, are close with family and friends, and have a normal social life. Most Ásatrúar are not a member of an Ásatrú organization, choosing instead to practice with close friends and family. They may celebrate personal, seasonal, and annual rituals. Some may not engage in rituals at all. Ásatrúar originate from all walks of life; they are rich and poor, urban and rural; they belong to many different cultures, races, ethnicities, and genders.

PRACTICING ÁSATRÚ TODAY

Thor's hammer pendants are a very important symbol for many Ásatrúar and heathens. Carrying Thor's hammer around your neck can make you feel closer to the gods and give you a sense of safety and stability in your daily life. It is a great way to connect with your spirituality on a daily basis, and it is also a great way to connect with other heathens. Most Ásatrúar are familiar with the Thor's hammer pendant and they will certainly recognize it if they see you wearing it. The Viking Age museums in Denmark, Iceland, Norway, and Sweden sell replicas of Thor's hammer pendants in bronze, silver, and gold through their online museum stores. They are fashioned after replicas of hammers that Vikings actually wore.

CHAPTER TWO

BEING ÁSATRÚ TODAY

There are many ways that you can live your life as Ásatrúar or heathen in the modern world. It all comes down to your personal feelings about spirituality and your imagination regarding the expression of that spirituality. Look deep inside yourself and ask, "What do I need from life and how can the gods and spirits help me find it?" The most important thing to remember is that, no matter what you believe or how you choose to practice, *you* are in control and decide your own luck and fate.

ÁSATRÚ WORLDVIEW

Do you believe that Thor drives a chariot through the sky and creates thunder? I've been asked this very question countless times by people when they've found out that I am heathen. I doubt that there are many heathens in the world who actually believe that thunder comes from a god that rides a chariot in the sky, but it is often how people view heathen beliefs: as curious, childlike superstition. The background for such belief is, naturally, the conversion to Christianity in Europe, where Christianity was promoted as the true faith and contrasted against non-Christian beliefs. The non-Christian beliefs were first demonized and then later ridiculed. In the era of Enlightenment, Christianity, whether Catholic or Protestant, received a similar treatment of ridicule by those who believed only in science and reason. The truth about belief, however, is that it comes in many different shapes and sizes, all of which are unique and valid. To understand the difference between belief in Ásatrú and the major world religions, one must understand that neither Ásatrú (the religion itself) nor any leaders or founders ever required anyone to *believe*. Asking the question "Do you believe in (the) god(s)?" does not actually make much sense to heathens. Instead of talking about belief, heathens would say that they have a certain *worldview*.

"Lore"

The many different beings that heathens believe in are the subject of stories and epics in Norse literature. Snorri Sturluson's *Edda* and the Eddic poems are incredibly important texts for heathens. So is much of the saga literature, not least the folklore of Scandinavia. Myths and legends give heathens the foundation for understanding the heathen worldview. Scandinavians grow up with the stories, learning about them in school and from their parents telling them folktales and stories about the Norse gods. In the Scandinavian landscape, there remain burial mounds that date back to the Viking Age, the Bronze Age, and the Stone Age, all of which are protected by law. Most Scandinavians are used to thinking of those buried within the mounds as "ancestors," even if they themselves are not a practicing heathen.

In the same way, modern Scandinavians feel a connection to their past by visiting runestones carved by Vikings, the Bronze Age rock-carvings, and various natural features in the landscape which are tied to well-known stories. Scandinavians today still, to some degree, understand the place-names that were dedicated to the Norse gods long ago, most of which are still in use. The famous Danish fairytale author Hans Christian Andersen, who wrote the *Little Mermaid* and the *Ugly Duckling*, came from Odense, a large city in Denmark, whose name means *Óðinn's Temple*. When Shakespeare wrote *Hamlet*, he took the name of an ancient Danish king, Amleð, and turned him into a dramatic prince in Elsinore Castle. The castle exists, but, more important, so does Amleð's grave. The grave is down the road from where my family is from, and we have often gone there to honor the old hero's memory. In the same manner, as Scandinavians travel through their home countries, they can identify places from the ancient stories and take time to venerate them. Many of the places have markers, street signs, or even statues of gods and heroes. The ancient heathen past is still recognized as integral to modern culture, even if the majority of modern Scandinavians are Christian.

Heathens in North America do not have the same opportunity to go out into their landscape and locate the ancient stories like Scandinavians can. As a result, the literature typically feels more distant to those living outside of Scandinavia. Over the years, I have seen many American heathens treating the ancient stories as scripture, as is done with the Christian Bible. In American Ásatrú, people tend to call the stories "lore," but the ancient stories were never meant to be read as if they contained the whole truth about the world. When they were written down, they were written by people who did not believe in the Norse gods and spirits. Before that, the stories were told by way of an oral culture, where people knew that there was no such thing as firm truth in any tale.

So, while heathens, and Scandinavians in particular, do not view the stories as "lore," they do regard them as an expression of a *worldview*: They are one way of seeing the world, among a multitude of other ways.

Fate and Luck

In the ancient stories, we learn that the world and humans are fated. Some of the stories feature the *nornir*, the female spirits of fate, and while nobody knows exactly how many there are, three of them are mentioned by Snorri Sturluson and in the Eddic poem *Vøluspá* (The *Vølva*'s Prophecy): Urðr, Verðandi, and Skuld. The nornir live by the well called Urðarbrunnr at the foot of Yggdrasill, the tree that stands in the middle of the world and represents the cosmos. An eagle sits in its crown and a serpent lies among its roots; time flows as water through the tree, and from the crown falls the dew and rain, which flows over the world's soil and collects in the well. These three *nornir* control the fate of humans and the world. The three nornir, Urðr, Verðandi, and Skuld, represent the past, present, and future. They weave threads of fate for humans, tie them in the tree, and cut them when it is time. Skuld cuts rune-sticks for each human to set their fate and lifespan.

It is believed that individuals are fated from the day they are born. *Gipta*, *gæfu*, and *hammingja* are three very important words in Ásatrú. *Gipta* is that which has been given to you from birth, while *gæfu* is your personal ability. *Hammingja* is the total sum of all that you have, what you make of it, and what the world bestows on you. The word *hammingja* comes from the word *hamr*, which means "body-shroud." It literally has to do with your appearance: how you look to others. In the modern English language, hammingja is similar to referring to one's personal carriage or how someone carries themselves ("He carries himself well").

Ørlög is another important word to know. It means "ancient law," and it describes the confluence of events that preceded gipta. Think of it as threads in a web that all tie together to become a string: *your* string. Every human has ørlög. You received it in the creation. *Bors synir*, the sons of Bor, are the three creator gods who made humans from trees in the dawn of time. Sometimes, the Bors synir are called Óðinn, Vili, and Vé, at other times they are known as Óðinn, Hœnir, and Lóðurr or Óðinn, Hœnir, and Loki. *Vøluspá* reveals how it all happened:

*"Fundo á landi, lítt megandi, Asc oc Emblo, ørlöglausa. Önd
þau né átto, óð þau né höfðo, lá né læti né lito góða; önd gaf
Óðinn, óð gaf Hœnir, lá gaf Lóðurr oc lito góða."*

("They found Askr and Embla on the land, powerless and without *ørlög*.
They had no spirit, no mind, no color, nor the gifts of life; Óðinn gave
spirit, Hœnir gave mind, Lóðurr/Loki gave color and the gifts of life.")

Ørlög is the gift of life that came from the gods. *Gipta* is that which is
given to you from your family line. *Gæfu* are the abilities you harness
yourself. Together, they combine to become *hammingja*, the way you carry
yourself in life. The sum of all the components is your luck in life. Some
believe that the gods are very involved in the process, while others believe
that you are left to your own devices in shaping your luck and your future.
In the old stories, especially in the sagas, there are two kinds of people:
those who believed they were fated and could do nothing about it, and
those who believed in their own power and ability. Often, in the sagas,
a person's fate appears to them as a *dís*, a goddess that follows you and
your family.

GODS AND GODDESSES

There are many words in Norse and modern Scandinavian for the gods,
goddesses, and other beings. The most common one in Norse is *óss/áss* in
the singular (sg.) and *æsir* in the plural (pl.). There is also *van* (sg.)/*vanir* (pl.),
which is most commonly used to refer to the fertility deities Freyr, Freyja,
and Njörðr/Nerþus. In modern Scandinavian, outside Iceland, the words
are spelled *as/ås* (sg.), *aser/åser/æser* (pl.), *van* (sg.) and *vaner* (pl.).

Ásatrúar and heathens generally worship the Norse gods, but it is
important to understand that their worship is not limited only to the gods
mentioned in the old texts written in Scandinavia. Aside from the Norse
pantheon, Ásatrúar also worship Germanic deities such as the Old English
Ēostre, the Saxon Seaxnot, the Central German Vraa Holle, and many
others. The gods mentioned in Snorri's *Edda* and the Eddic poems are only

a minor collection of the total sum of deities and beings that heathens worship. If all of the different local deities are counted that exist in the Germanic and Scandinavian traditions, there are more than 1,000 gods and spirits.

As polytheists, heathens are not necessarily exclusive in their relationship to deities. Some may include deities from other cultures in their personal worship. There can be many reasons for doing so. Some do it because they live in a place where a particular deity is considered most important or powerful, others do it because they have personal ancestry in other traditions, and yet others do it because at some point in life, they cultivated a personal relationship with a deity from another tradition. Historically, doing so is very common in nearly all polytheistic traditions. For instance, deities like the Egyptian Isis and the Middle Eastern Dionysus and the Persian Mithras, along with many Celtic deities, were worshipped by Germanic peoples in the Rhineland area. In Scandinavia, Finnish and Sámi deities also overlap heavily with the Norse ones. In the following sections, you will find an overview of some of the more popular deities among Ásatrúar today.

Óðinn

Óðinn (*Odin, Woden, Wotan*) is a very popular god to whom many Ásatrúar relate. Many see him as "the All-father," although this is a misunderstanding of his original nature. Snorri is responsible for having portrayed Óðinn as an All-father in *Edda*, essentially interpreting him as a heathen version of the Christian god in the Bible. Scholars of Norse literature are well aware of this, but the knowledge has not necessarily reached the broad public. In Scandinavia, few see Óðinn as an All-father, but to many American Ásatrúar, he is revered as just that. The reason is probably that many Americans have grown up with a somewhat authoritarian version of Christianity, and when they find Ásatrú, they seek familiarity in the heathen spirituality. However, it is markedly different in Scandinavia, where few have the same ideas of religious authorities as in North America.

Historically, Óðinn is a god of war, death, mystery, knowledge, wisdom, runes, and magic, and thus, he was important to kings and warriors alike during the Viking Age. Warriors could harness his power in battle and use his magic, turning themselves into *úlfheðnar* (wolf) and *berserkir* (bear) warriors. Óðinn was a guide in rituals, letting the *þulr* or *vǫlva* channel the spirit-world as they communicated with him. His principal animals are eagles, ravens, and wolves. Óðinn himself appears as an eagle, but his mind and memory, *huginn* and *muninn*, fly across the world as ravens. His darker side manifests itself as the greedy and aggressive wolves *geri* and *freki*.

The truth is that a follower of Ásatrú should be very careful with creating close bonds with Óðinn. He is not the caring, reliable god that many believe him to be. Everything that he gives comes with a price.

Frigg

Frigg (*Frigga*), Óðinn's wife, is often thought of as a queen for the same reason as Óðinn is believed to be a kinglike All-father. She is a mother-goddess who cares for her children, and many heathen women look to her for guidance in such matters. She is also the warden of the secret wisdom of women, and she resides in the marsh halls called *Fensalir*. In that sense, she has a hand in fate and can be good to call upon for matters that have to do with your family's luck. Frigg will often appear in the myths as a swan.

Þórr

Þórr (*Thor, Tor*) is and has always been the most popular of the Norse gods. In Norse literature, he is called *miðgarðs verjandi*, the "protector of Earth"; his hammer pendants were incredibly popular during the Viking Age, and he is often invoked in runic inscriptions from that period, where the words *þur uiki* (Þórr hallow) are used as a protection spell. He is a god of strength, power, protection, masculinity, and also a warden of fertility and safety from illness. He is undoubtedly the most popular god among modern Ásatrúar, and he is also the least misunderstood. The way that modern heathens see Þórr, and the way in which they relate to him today, is probably not that far from how he was seen by the ancient heathens.

Sif

Sif is often worshipped as a fertility goddess who has control over the growth cycle of plants, specifically the crops of the field. While there is very little information about her in the Norse texts, Ásatrúar today see her golden hair as a representation of the ripe grains in the field. The interpretation likely stems from a story in Snorri's *Edda*, where Loki cuts off Sif's golden hair. Scholars in the late 19th century interpreted the story as a symbolic tale of the fertility of the crops in the field. Sif represents the crops, and her husband, Þórr, the thunder-god in charge of the summer rains, represents the fertility force that makes her ripen. She is a very potent image in agricultural traditions and certainly one that even city-dwelling Ásatrúar can relate to.

Baldr

Baldr (*Balder, Baldur*) is the tragic son of Frigg, who dies by the hand of his brother Höðr, tricked by Loki. He is as misunderstood in modern Ásatrú as Óðinn, due to late 19th century interpretations by scholars that argued that Baldr was either a sun-god or a Christlike figure. Both interpretations are incorrect but have gained some popularity in modern Ásatrú. Baldr is not the sun-god. The goddess *Sól*, whose name means "sun," is the sun-god. Neither is Baldr a Norse version of Christ. His story is much older than Christianity's influence on Northern Europe, and it has very little to do with the idea of a god who suffers for our sins. However, the interpretation of Baldr as Christ is not completely unwarranted if you read Snorri's *Edda* and truly believe that Óðinn, Baldr's father, is a godlike "all-father." That is likely what scholars in the 19th century did, because they did not understand the difference between Christian and non-Christian myth.

The historical Baldr is the god of male prowess. He represents all the good and beautiful virtues of a harmonious, well-balanced, and physically capable young man. His name means "hero," and he is the warden of all young men who aspire to do great deeds.

Loki

Loki is perhaps the most misrepresented, misinterpreted, and misunderstood of the gods. As with the misunderstandings and misinterpretations surrounding Óðinn and Baldr, the misconceptions about Loki come from a literal and uncritical way of reading Snorri's *Edda*. Taken at face value, Snorri's *Edda* represents Óðinn as "God," Baldr as "Christ," Frigg as "Mother Mary," and Loki as "Judas" (or maybe even "Satan"). This was likely part of Snorri's intention of making Norse mythology look like misunderstood Christianity. The problem today is that the backstory is not obvious to modern Ásatrúar, who read the old stories as "lore" and "scripture."

Loki belongs to the very common group of gods across the world who function as tricksters. They are the ones who create problems for the other gods, sometimes devastating problems, but there is always a creative element to their mischief. The tricksters are the reason that inventions and useful tools are developed by gods and humans alike. For instance, Prometheus brought fire to humans by stealing it from Zeus. Similarly, Loki cut Sif's hair, but he brought the hammer to Þórr, the spear to Óðinn, the ship to Freyr and Njörðr, and he invented the fishing net.

Religious beliefs have followed the same trend for centuries. The Native American trickster-god Coyote was turned into a fearsome devil by Christian missionaries. The same happened with Eshú in the Yoruba tradition in West Africa. Originally, neither of them was a "devil," but in the meeting with a religion that sets strong boundaries between good and bad, they become negative figures. The same happened to Loki some 1,000 years ago, when Christianity spread to the North. A creative and innovative fire-god was turned into a dangerous devil. However, there are also many who worship Loki in different ways. I always make sure to give Loki rum and salt before I make an offering to any other god.

Freyja

Freyja (*Freya, Freja, Freia*)—very popular among Ásatrúar, especially women—is the goddess of love and sexuality. She not only represents female sexual energy; she also represents female aggression and force. Her name means "lady," and she is often represented as a beautiful woman or with a depiction of a vulva. She is a warden of the special kinds of ritual magic called *seiðr*. In mythology, she can appear as a hawk, a falcon, or a cat.

Freyr

Freyr (*Frey, Frej*) is Freyja's brother and represents the male force complementary to Freyja's female sexuality. Freyr is traditionally represented with an erect penis, and he is associated with the boar and the horse. Ásatrúar today see him as an important god for male sexuality, lovemaking, and marriage.

Iðunn

Iðunn (*Idun*) is a youth-goddess and responsible for the eternal return, which manifests in the cycle of the year. The cycle of the year goes from spring to winter, but it is much more than that: It is the cycle of life in a cosmic sense. *Iðunn* means "eternal one," and she is a youth and renewal force for humans, the seasons, and the world itself.

Skaði

Skaði (*Skathi, Skadi*) is raw female energy. She is a ski-goddess, huntress associated with wolves, and a mountain warrior. She rules the woods and mountains and is a good friend to any person who enjoys the deep woods and tall mountains.

Týr

Týr is a god of war. In the old stories, he sacrifices his hand to the wolf Fenrir for the good of his community, just as any proper warrior would. He represents the greatest sacrifice a warrior can make for their community, as well as values such as honor, fealty, and courage.

Eir

Eir is the goddess of healing and medicine. Many modern Ásatrúar worship her for good health and healing. Heathens tend to look to her for comfort and protection, or for help when they or a family member is sick.

Hel

Hel (*Hella*) is the goddess of the realm of the dead called Niflhel or Niflheim. She welcomes all the dead there and cares for them. She is also a powerful goddess for *seiðr*-magic. Some Ásatrúar are not so comfortable worshipping her, but there are many who are.

Njörðr

Njörðr (*Njord, Niord*) is Freyr and Freyja's father, the god of ships and the bounties of sea. Many sailors put their trust in him to help them on their ocean journeys.

Jörð

Jörð (*Jord*) is the goddess of Earth, and she is Þórr's mother. Many Ásatrúar today see her as the Norse representation of the Mother Earth Goddess.

Sól and Máni

Sól and Máni are sister and brother. Sól, sometimes also called Sunna, is the goddess of the sun. Her brother Máni is the god of the moon. Many Ásatrúar hold them very dear and worship them in different ways.

RELATIONSHIPS WITH THE GODS

Some believe the gods are as real as humans, while others believe they are symbols of ideas, values, forces, and feelings. Some believe they are both. Some believe you can contact the gods and have close relationships with them, while others believe that the gods do not really care about humans but are more interested in the greater cosmic processes. Heathens usually say that there are as many ways of seeing the gods as there are heathens in the world. A wise old Danish heathen named Ole Gotved once said it this way:

> *"Gudernes ansigt ingen kender. Vi laver et billede som ligner os selv. Vi ser det samme men ser forskelligt, ingen kan sige hvis syn er sandest."*

("Nobody knows the faces of the gods. We make an image that looks like us. We see the same, but we see it differently, none know whose sight sees truth.")

Gods or Archetypes?

Do the gods live and exist the same way as humans? Do they breathe and walk among us? Some heathens certainly think so. Some heathens see the gods in the crowds of humans on the street, on buses or in the subway, in the mountains and trees, in the lakes, in the ocean, in the sky, in every animal and movement of a blade of grass.

Other heathens see the gods as archetypes of basic emotions and aspects of the human condition, which exist within us but not outside of us. The idea of archetypes comes from the Swiss psychologist Carl Gustav Jung (1875 to 1961), who famously used Norse mythology to write about the shared subconscious processes in the human brain. Many Ásatrúar see Jung as somewhat of a heathen philosopher, who proposed a way of believing in the gods in the modern world.

Personally, I see the gods as entities that inhabit our world just like humans. You can find them out there, wherever you want, and you can make up your own mind about who and what they are.

Fulltrúi and Ástvinr

In the old stories, there are different ways of expressing a close relationship to a god. *Fulltrúi* is a Norse word that means "encompassing dedication." In *Hrafnkels saga Freysgoði*, the chieftain Hrafnkell is the fulltrúi of the god Freyr. Hrafnkell is goði of a temple he builds in honor of Freyr alone, and he dedicates his horse to this god, too, calling it Freyfaxi (Freyr's Mane). As such, it is an example of how ancient heathens could have close relationships to gods. In modern Ásatrú, there are many who call themselves the fulltrúi of a certain deity, typically one whose temper and perspective on the world reflects their own. The implication of being fulltrúi, however, is a sense of henotheism, where the fulltrúi exclusively worships one god without believing that this is the only god in existence. Such exclusivity does not sit well with many heathens.

A less common way of having a personal relationship to a deity is to cultivate a connection that is called being a god's *ástvinr*. Ástvinr means "loving friend" and signifies that a person has a dear and close relationship to a certain god, who is seen as their friend. You may be the ástvinr of Þórr, for instance, if you have a close personal relationship to him but do not refrain from worshipping the other gods.

JÖTNAR AND TROLLS

The words *jötunn* (sg.)/*jötnar* (pl.), *þurs* (sg.)/*þursar*, and *troll* (sg.)/*tröll* (pl.) are used for demonic beings. In modern Scandinavia outside of Iceland, they are referred to as *jette/jœtte/jätte/jotne/jotun* (sg.), *jetter/jœtter/jätter/jotner/jotnar* (pl.), *troll/trold* (sg.), and *troller/trolde* (pl.).

It is most certain that, from the dawn of time, the jötnar and trolls have been considered threats to human existence. They are the counterpart to the gods, and they represent chaotic forces in the world, but they are not evil. While you will certainly get the idea that they are evil from reading Snorri's Christianized account of Norse mythology in *Edda*, it is important to understand that there are many different kinds of relationships between the æsir, álfar, vanir, jötnar, dísir, dvergar, and all the other beings that exist in our world. Many heathens worship different jötnar and trolls, too. Some do it because they respect their powers, while others do it because they seek to instigate chaos.

ANCESTORS AND SPIRITS

Ancestor worship is incredibly important to many heathens. In Scandinavia, the ancestors are evident everywhere one views the landscape. In North America and outside of Scandinavia, many worship ancestors because it ties them to Scandinavia and to the world from which part of their heritage comes. Nordic and Germanic tribes migrated across Europe during ancient times, and people from Northern Europe have migrated to other parts of the world during modern times, thus resulting in people all across the world with Germanic and Scandinavian heritage. However, you do not need to have Germanic and Scandinavian heritage to be Ásatrú, to be heathen, or to worship your ancestors. It is natural for all humans to care for their distant mothers and fathers through rituals. Many heathens communicate with their ancestors in ceremonies and forge strong bonds with their ancient relatives as they continue to protect and guide us.

Ásatrú is in many ways an animist tradition, where the world is believed to be inhabited by different spirits. The word *álfr* (sg.)/*álfar* (pl.) is used for fertility-spirits. *Dís* (sg.)/*dísir* (pl.) is a common word for female fate-spirits. *Dvergr* (sg.)/*dvergar* (pl.) is used for certain minor demonic spirits that live in the ground. The many different local spirits are just as important for heathens as the gods themselves. The following sections list some of the most important spirits in Norse mythology and in Scandinavian folklore.

Álfar, Huldur, Vættir, and *Landvættir*

In modern Scandinavian, these beings are known as *alf/alv/elv/älv* (sg.), *alfer/alver/alvar/elver/älver* (pl.), *huldur/hulder/huldrer*, and (land-)*vetter/ vætter/vätter*. They are spirits of a local site. They live in rocks, trees, mounds, and other features of the landscape. They protect the land, and it is always a good idea to stay on good terms with them. In Scandinavian folklore, they are responsible for pushing people off cliffs or harming those who cross them. Often, they can be appeased with libations: pour out mead or beer for them. In many places in Scandinavia, Ásatrúar have a tradition of giving the last part of the mead in a ceremony to the *landvættir*. Many in Scandinavia still believe in the existence of these beings, even if they are not heathens.

Dísir

In modern Scandinavia, these are called *dis* (sg.), *diser/disir/disar* (pl.). The *dísir* are protective spirits of your family. Everyone has one and she follows you around, whether you like it or not. She is your most ancient mother and she wishes you the best of luck, so make sure that you stay on good terms with her.

Nisse, Tomte, Gardvord, and *Tunkall*

Every house has a *nisse, tomte, gardvord,* or *tunkall*. They are called different things across Scandinavia, but no matter the name, they are the same kind of being: a protective spirit. They live with you and are responsible for whether things go right or wrong in your house. Caring for the *nisse* is one of the most enduring traditions in Scandinavia. Even modern non-heathens in Scandinavia believe in the *nisse*. In some places, you put out a bowl of porridge for the *nisse* on Yule Eve, while in other places you have to make a plate for him and keep an empty seat and an empty bed for him during Yule. Many heathens today give the *nisse* offerings on a regular basis to keep the peace in their house.

Dvergar

These are called *dverg/dværg/dvärg* (sg.), *dverger/dvergar/dværge/dvärger* (pl.) in modern Scandinavia. In ancient times, they were believed to be responsible for illness. They are demons in the ground who come up at night and bite the fingers of children. Some heathens still practice magic to keep them away. They live in rocks and can sometimes trick people into following them into their rock, never to be seen again.

Skogsrå, Ellepike, Nøkken, Sælfolk, Havfolk, and Draugar

The *skogsrå* is a demon that inhabits the woods and steals people's *hugr* (mind) by tricking them into telling him their name. The *ellepike* is a beautiful woman who greets travelers on the road at night, but when they embrace her, they realize that she is in fact a tree demon who takes them into water and drowns them. *Nøkken* is a particular spirit of the water who will often make a bargain with musicians: He takes your hugr in exchange for musical talents. The *sælfolk* are a special kind of people who live in the ocean in the guise of seals. They are very similar to *havfolk*, the spirits of the drowned sailors. You should treat them with respect and care for them. The havfolk will ask you for help, and you should give it to them. That will ensure safe passage. The sælfolk, on the other hand, should be left alone unless they come to you. The *draugar* are the spirits of those who died gruesome and violent deaths. They are lingering ghosts who haunt the places where they died.

HUGR, HAMR, FYLGJA

Heathens do not believe in a soul in the same way as Christians and Muslims. The old Scandinavian concept of "soul" is hugr, which (as mentioned) means "mind." Everyone has a hugr, even animals and natural features, such as trees, rocks, rivers, and others. The hugr has a *hamr*, a "body-shroud" or, literally, "skin." You can take on another hamr if you have the power to do it—that is, if you know magic like *seiðr* or *galdr*. Your hugr lives inside you, but it is not uncommon that a person's hugr can appear as their *fylgja* when they sleep. The fylgja is the projection of a person's individual qualities in animal form. Everyone has a fylgja, an animal that represents them. When a person comes of age, it is customary to take them on a journey to find their fylgja.

THE AFTERLIFE

Some care about life after death, others do not. That the ancient heathens believed in an afterlife that was quite literally the same as the life they had lived is apparent from Viking Age graves. People were buried with all kinds of items and goods, including horses, dogs, slaves, weapons, and precious items like gold jewelry. In the old stories, there are mentions of Hel's underworld *Niflhel* and Óðinn's warrior heaven *Valhøll*. Many modern heathens know Snorri's very Christian representation of this from *Edda*, where the descriptions of Valhøll give us the sense that it is a meat-filled and booze-fueled warrior party, while those who did not die in battle languish in boredom in Hel's dreary underworld. Many modern heathens, especially in North America, latch on to this idea, thinking that it somehow makes sense that one's ancestors were so bloodthirsty that they came up with these ideas about the afterlife.

However, that is not the case, and most Scandinavian heathens think that such ideas pertaining to the afterlife are ridiculous. Scholars are also well aware that Snorri's descriptions of Valhøll and Niflhel are almost direct copies of medieval Christian ideas of heaven and hell, and very similar to Dante's *Divine Comedy*. Snorri's main source for representing Valhøll as a warrior paradise is the Eddic poem *Grímnismál* (The Masked One's Speech), which describes the death realm of warriors figuratively as such a hall but in fact says that the warriors die under the open sky. Most heathens who are aware of this do not give much thought to what kind of place they go to when they die. Instead, they are focused on how they live their life now. Focusing on your lived life and its legacy is a central part of modern heathen beliefs that resonates directly with what Óðinn says in stanza 76 to 77 of *Hávamál* (The Speech of High):

"Deyr fé, deyia frœndr, deyr siálfr it sama; enn orðztírr deyr aldregi, hvem er sér gódan getr. Deyr fé, deyia frœndr, deyr siálfr it sama; ec veit einn, at aldri deyr: dómr um dauðan hvern."

("Cattle die, family dies, you die yourself all the same; but praise never dies for those who get a good reputation. Cattle die, family dies, you die yourself all the same; I know something that never dies: people's judgment of every dead person.")

Modern and ancient heathens alike have always been more preoccupied with leaving a good reputation behind, rather than worrying about an afterlife. The famous heathen musician Einar Selvik, of the Norwegian band Wardruna, expresses the heathen thoughts of the afterlife in the song *Helvegen* (*The Hel-road*):

"Kven skal synge meg, i daudsvevna slynge meg, når eg på Helvegen går og dei spora eg trår er kalde, så kalde?"

("Who will sing for me, wrap me in death-sleep, when I walk the Hel-road and those steps I walk are cold, so cold?")

That, if anything, is the extent of the heathen concern with the afterlife.

PRACTICING ÁSATRÚ TODAY

To get a sense of how the old heathen worldview looked, reading the old stories is important. You can find both the Eddic poems and Snorri's *Edda* in proper English translations. They are most often called the *Poetic Edda* and the *Prose Edda* in English. Take some time to read the stories about the different gods and see if there are one or more of them who speak to you. If any of the gods appeal to you, try to talk to them. You can create the space for doing that exactly in the way you want to. Don't be shy, and don't worry if you feel silly; that's okay!

CHAPTER THREE

ÁSATRÚ VALUES

There are many different Ásatrú groups across the world and their members have their origin in different cultures. Being Ásatrú and heathen is not uniform or limited in terms of values. Keep in mind that Ásatrú is a non-dogmatic community spirituality: It does not have texts that are used as scripture. Its beliefs and values come from the community that it has its root in, and followers cherish independence and individuality. A wise woman named Silje Herup Juvet, one of the founders of Ásatrufellesskapet Bifrost in Norway, once said to me: *I believe in the values of Norwegian society. That is because I am Ásatrú and Norway is my community. Community and society come first!*

Strong respect for society and community is something that many heathens value. In Scandinavia, heathens often refer to Þorgeirr Ljósvetningagoði—the heathen man who was law-speaker at the Icelandic general assembly in the year 1000 CE, when Iceland converted to Christianity—to demonstrate how the heathen tradition prioritizes law and social integrity. When he saw how religious strife was tearing society apart, he decided that Iceland should follow Christian law.

He said:

"Þat mon verða satt, es vér slítum í sundr lǫgin, at vér monum slíta ok friðinn."

("It will prove true that if we tear apart the laws, we will also tear apart the peace.")

THE *HÁVAMÁL*

While heathens do not follow scripture and dogma, they are fond of the ancient stories and how they can suggest strong core values and offer guidance to those seeking to live good lives. The *Hávamál* (The Speech of High) is an important text pertaining to that. It is the longest Eddic poem, comprising 164 stanzas, and it is said to be the words of Óðinn himself. Heathens usually regard what Óðinn says in the poem as good advice for living one's life. The first 80 stanzas of the poem are advice on how to act around other people. Óðinn addresses themes such as hospitality, intelligence, social conduct, friendship, money and possessions, personal capabilities, and family. I will give a brief overview of the values that *Hávamál* expresses, but I strongly advise that you read the poem on your own and to come to your own conclusion on its message and meaning.

Hospitality

The first stanzas in *Hávamál* talk about hospitality and being a good host and a good guest. The host should be generous to their guests and offer food, drink, warmth, and good conversation. A guest should be courteous and cautious, respect the rules of the house they are in, and be considerate of not insulting others.

Intelligence

Be smart! In stanza 11, Óðinn says:

"Byrði betri berrat maðr brauto at, enn sé manvit mikit."

("A man carries no better burden than a good portion of common sense.")

There are many stanzas in *Hávamál* that are dedicated to wisdom, knowledge, and competence. Do not overindulge; do not mock others; do not argue with a fool; do not spend too much; do not let good things go to waste and squander life; do not worry too much; and do not act like a smartass, because you never know if you are in the company of someone who is smarter than you! Often, violence and revenge come out of a situation where someone violates this advice. Ancient Scandinavians believed that intelligence and wisdom were important gifts. They were also well aware that a person who is actually intelligent does not boast about it.

Etiquette and Behavior

A person who boasts has never been particularly charming. As a Scandinavian saying goes, "Empty barrels make the loudest noises!" Óðinn values the virtue of humility highly, and he is not fond of brooding and grumpy types. Instead, he encourages joyfulness mixed with a portion of restraint. He suggests that you lay off greed and excessive eating habits in stanza 20. Moderation is key, according to Óðinn. Do not eat or drink excessively, do not talk too much, and do not ever expect that you are safe from harm. According to Óðinn, idiots lie awake at night and worry about when they will die, and idiots show up in a place with a chip on their shoulder.

Stanzas 16 and 17 state:

"Ósniallr maðr hyggz muno ey lifa, ef hann við víg varaz; enn elli gefr hánom engi frið, þótt hánom geirar gefi. Kópir afglapi, er til kynnis kømr, þylsc hann um eða þrumir."

("An idiot believes they'll live forever if they avoid war; but age gives you no peace, regardless of what spears will grant. An idiot gawks [at people] when he comes to visit; he mumbles [about others] or acts foolish.")

Respect is another key. Show everyone around you respect and treat yourself and those around you with dignity. Do not mock others; do not gossip about others; do not overstay your welcome; and give a friendship time to grow—do not think that every person who smiles at you at the party is your friend.

Friendship

Óðinn has a lot to say about friendship. Stanza 34 begins with:

"Afhvarf mikit er til illz vinar, þótt á brauto búi!"

("It is a great detour to a bad friend, even if they live on your way!")

Óðinn advises you not to waste your time on people who are not really your friends. He mentions that he has never met a person who was so generous that they did not enjoy getting a gift, and he never met a person who was so liberal with their possessions that they did not happily take a reward. People, according to Óðinn, should be generous to one another, but you should not waste your generosity on people who do not appreciate it.

Óðinn is clear when it comes to friendship and loyalty, as is evidenced in stanzas 43 to 44:

"Vin sínom scal maðr vinr vera, þeim oc þess vin; enn óvinar síns scyli engi maðr vinar vinr vera. Veiztu ef þú vin átt, þann er þú vel trúir, oc vill þú af hánom gott geta: geði scaltu við þann blanda oc giöfom scipta, fara at finna opt."

("You should be a friend to your friend, and to your friend's friend, but none should be a friend to their un-friend's friend. You know, if you have a friend that you trust and want good things of them: You must mix your thoughts with them and exchange gifts and go visit them often!")

Friendship does not come easy. It is something that you must work for and never take for granted. If a friendship is true, you will know that you can speak your mind to your friend, and they can do the same to you.

Wealth and Possessions

Self-reliance is certainly an important value in Ásatrú, and it is echoed by Óðinn in *Hávamál*, specifically in stanzas 36 to 37:

"Bú er betra, þótt lítit sé, halr er heima hverr; þótt tvær geitir eigi oc taugreptan sal, þat er þó betra en bœnn. Bú er betra, þótt lítit sé, halr er heima hverr; blóðuct er hiarta, þeim er biðia scal sér í mál hvert matar."

("A house is better, even if it is small, everyone is a hero at home; to have two goats and a poorly thatched hall—that is better than begging. A house is better, even if it is small, everyone is a hero at home; anyone who must beg for food for every meal does so with a bleeding heart.")

The script has two meanings: On the one hand, he is encouraging everyone to be self-reliant; on the other hand, he is also making it clear that those who are not self-reliant do not fully enjoy life. There is also a reference to the importance of generosity. In stanza 47, Óðinn emphasizes sharing:

"Ungr var ec forðom, fór ec einn saman, þá varð ec villr vega; auðigr þóttomz, er ec annan fann, maðr er mannz gaman."

("Young I was in ancient times, when I traveled alone and became lost; I thought that I was rich when I found someone else, humanity is humanity's joy.")

As humans we should be kind and generous to one another. This is the most important virtue, according to Óðinn. We are fools if we think that we can go it alone; we need each other, even if we are strangers. However, Óðinn also cautions against squandering your possessions. In stanza 49, he says:

"Váðir mínar gaf ec velli at tveim trémönnom; reccar þat þóttuz, er þeir rift höfðo, neiss er nøcqviðr halr."

("I gave my garbs to two tree-men on an open plain; they looked like warriors as they posed with the clothes, shame on a naked fool!")

It is all about balance: Do not be too generous, but do not be greedy either! Óðinn has good advice on how to keep a good balance in stanza 52:

"Mikit eitt scala manni gefa, opt kaupir sér í litlo lof; með hálfom hleif oc með höllo keri fecc ec mér félaga."

("There is no need for great gifts alone, even a little will buy praise; with half a loaf and a half-empty cup, I got myself a friend.")

Genuine generosity is difficult to master. People will give too much to impress others, and often it is a way to convince others that they are wealthy and capable human beings. However, in Scandinavian culture, such behavior has never been perceived as flattering. To Scandinavians, if you attempt to impress them with your possessions, you will appear fake. Most know that there are strings attached to an expensive gift, and most also know that if someone gives expensive gifts, it is because he or she does not have more to offer than their money.

Personal Capabilities

In stanza 62, Óðinn describes a person who does not know the measure of things:

"Snapir oc gapir, er til sævar kømr, örn á aldinn mar; svá er maðr, er með mörgom kømr oc á formælendr fá."

("The eagle gasps and stretches its neck when it comes to the ancient sea; just like the man who goes to the assembly and finds that he has few to speak for him.")

Personal capabilities are incredibly important virtues in Ásatrú. A sleeping wolf seldom gets the deer! You should get up early and work, and you should see to it that you have enough in your storage. You must know how to ask and answer; maintain moderation; be on time; keep good hygiene, even if your clothes are old.

Everyone has value, as Óðinn says in stanzas 71 and 75:

"Haltr ríðr hrossi, hiörð recr handarvanr, daufr vegr oc dugir; blindr er betri, enn brendr sé: nytr mangi nás. Veita hinn, er vætki veit, margr verðr aflöðrom api; maðr er auðigr, annarr óauðigr scylit þann vitca vár."

("A limping person can ride a horse, the handless guides a herd, the deaf may fight well; it is better to be blind than to be burned: there is no use for a corpse. He knows who knows nothing, many are monkeys for cash; one person is rich, another is poor, don't blame him for that.")

Óðinn's advice is clear. There is always use for a person; no one is useless, and no one should be cast aside for their faults. The same is true for one's physical attributes as much as for wealth and class. Everyone deserves respect. Óðinn is well aware that wealth is fleeting—it is like a twinkle of an eye, the ficklest of friends. You may think that you have it made, but do not let that go to your head.

Family

Happiness comes with being loved by family and loving your family back. A good, supportive family life is everything. This is expressed by Óðinn in stanza 50:

"Hrørnar þöll, sú er stendr þorpi á, hlyra henni börcr né barr; svá er maðr, sá er mangi ann, hvat scal hann lengi lifa?"

("The fir-tree that stands on the bare hill dwindles, bark and thorns give no shelter; that is like the person that no one loves, why should they live long?")

In *Egil's Saga*, the ancient Viking Egill Skallagrímsson recites a tragic lament for the death of his son. This lament was called *Sonatorrek*, or the *Loss of the Son*. In stanza 6, Egill describes family in the following way:

"Grimt vörum hlið, þats hrönn of braut föður míns á frænd-garði; veitk ófult ok opit standa sonar skarð, es mér sœr of vann."

("It's a grim sight to see, the hole that the sea shot in my family's fence; the sea took my son, and my son's post will always be open.")

Egill is describing how the sea took his son in a drowning accident. He uses an analogy for his family, which is based on a fence. Every family member is a part of the fence that encircles the inner yard, the sanctum of every other family member; you guard every family member. This is sometimes referred to as *innangarðs* in Ásatrú. Your family is *innangarðs*, inside-the-fence; everything else is *útangarðs*, outside-the-fence. You are bound by loyalty to every person who exists *innangarðs*.

In the grand scheme of the mythology, this is also expressed in the home of the gods: Ásgarðr. Just like *innangarðs* is made of the words "inside" and "defensive rampart," so is the name for the home of the gods made of the words for "gods" and "defensive rampart": *áss + garðr*. The gods are a family that protects itself from the outside: Jötunheimr, the world of the *jötnar*.

Different rules apply to the inside and to the outside. You cannot expect to leave your family and home and find that everyone will act the same way as you are used to. That is why you are bound by loyalty to your family and only to your family. Loyalty to everyone else is a choice, and you should be cautious about making such choices, because it ultimately means that the loyalty bonds you make with others become the loyalty bonds of your family, too. The very last stanza (164) of *Hávamál* demonstrates the difference between inside and outside:

> *"Nú ero Háva mál qveðin, Háva höllo í, allþörf yta sonom, óþörf iötna sonom . . ."*

("Now, *Hávamál* has been uttered, in High's hall, useful for humans, not so useful for demons . . .")

Óðinn underlines that there are guidelines for you to use when you venture out into the world. If you follow them, you will have an easier time. They are not decrees, or laws, but rather they are guidelines of behavior and advice for how to best manage your life. You can choose to follow or disregard them. My best advice is to read *Hávamál* for yourself.

HONOR

Honor is an important value in Ásatrú. However, you should not think of honor in terms of something you can inherently *have*. Honor is earned and closely tied to personal worth. As a human being, you bring something to the table. You add value to a community. Your honor is directly linked to what you bring to the table, what value you have to your community.

So, where does that value come from? Your value is determined by how well you apply Óðinn's prescriptions for navigating life. Heathens will look at you and determine your honor based on how well you comport yourself. In its essence, "honor" comes from being responsible.

A responsible person is someone who makes sure to apply appropriate means to the different situations they find themselves in. Do not overdo it; do not neglect it—whatever it is. Many people mistakenly believe that the way the ancient Vikings of the saga literature handled their fights and feuds was honorable. However, what the Icelandic sagas teach us is that the blood feuds of ancient times were stupid and wasteful. In the sagas—and in the ancient laws of Scandinavia—a blood feud could come from nearly any little mistake. Most came from situations in which callous people overreacted with aggression. Such behavior is exactly the kind that Óðinn warns against in *Hávamál*. It is the person who is reluctant to start a feud who is the hero of any saga.

Preserving your honor—and, yes, that is important—depends on knowing when to act and understanding what measure should be applied. This knowledge comes only from being a wise person. It is not a universal rule that can be dictated from above. It all depends on how you will eventually be perceived by your peers. Remember: It is the judgment by others that determines if your reputation lives on after your death.

BONDS

We are all bound: to family, to friends, to animals, to the world, and to the gods. In the ancient poems, the gods are called *bönd* and *höpt*—*Bönd* means "the bonds" and *höpt* means "those who bind." Haptagoð, another name for Óðinn, means "the god who binds." All the powers in the world bind and all the powers in the world are bound to one another—gods and humans alike. We are all connected and we all have responsibility for one another. Any action can and will have the consequence of breaking or tightening a bond in the world.

The bonds are set and altered by the gods. Óðinn, as a ruler and war-god, has a strong role in this. Aside from being Haptagoð, he is also called Alföðr, Sigföðr, Herjaföðr/Herföðr, and Valföðr. These names are wrongly interpreted by Snorri Sturluson in *Edda* as "All-father, Victory-father, Army-father, and Father of the Slain," interpretations that have all too readily been adopted by many heathens. In reality, the names do not mean that Óðinn is the father of "all" or "the slain," and so on. The word -föðr actually means "the one who sets in order." By putting things in order, Óðinn is the one who bonds everything, bonds victory, bonds the army, and bonds the slain. What the names point to is his quality as a god of fate. He is not a father—there is nothing fatherly about him. Instead, he and the other gods bind the world in a fated, bonded community.

What does this mean for you? It means that you cannot escape the world's fate and the world's fate cannot escape you. Your actions have direct implications for everyone and everything else, and the actions of others have direct implications for you. No one is an island. No one can escape responsibility.

Many English-speaking Ásatrúar refer to this principle as Wyrd's Web. Wyrd is the name of the *norn* Urðr in Old English. In Scandinavia, she is called Urðr or Urd. People envision the web in many different ways, but what is important to understand is that it is the original way that heathens conceived of how fate and life weave everyone and everything together—all are part of the same whole.

What does that mean for a modern heathen? Think of this as the ripple effect or the butterfly effect. When you throw a stone in the water, it creates ripples across the surface; when a butterfly flaps its wings, it may set off a storm far away. As a human being, all your actions have consequences. You may not always feel and see the consequences immediately, but you should always expect that one bad deed breeds another. This is the same for good deeds. It is also the case for neutral deeds—or deeds that were never intended to be either good nor bad.

If you fish upstream, you may deprive someone downstream of fish. That is life, and for that reason, you should always consider your actions. You should always be mindful of all bonds, tying you to seen and unseen beings.

In the ancient stories, the myths, there are plenty of examples of how the gods bind the forces of chaos. The war-god and god of justice, Týr, bound the wolf Fenrir and sacrificed his hand in order to do so, but it was necessary. Binding Fenrir was an act of tethering chaos. According to the myths, the gods did the same to Loki when his chaotic side became too much by binding him in the underworld to prevent the cosmos from falling apart.

RAGNARØKK – RAGNARÖK

What makes the world fall apart? The world falls apart when we stop respecting the rules of life. Ásatrú does not prescribe strong rules and laws to live by, but there are a few things that the ancient heathens thought would bring on the destruction of the world. In stanzas 44 to 45 of *Vøluspá*, it says:

> *"Geyr Garmr miöc fyr Gnipahelli, festr mun slitna, enn freki renna; fiölð veit hon frœða, frem sé ec lengra um ragna röc, römm sigtyva. Brœðr muno beriaz oc at bönom verðaz, muno systrungar sifiom spilla; hart er í heimi, hórdómr mikill, sceggöld, scálmöld, scildir ro klofnir, vindöld, vargöld, áðr verold steypiz; mun engi maðr öðrom þyrma."*

("Garmr barks before Gnipahellir, his chain breaks, and the greedy runs; she knows much, I see ahead to Ragnarök, the darkness of the victory-gods. Brothers will fight and kill each other, siblings will destroy their bonds; it's hard in the world, there is much whoredom, axe-age, sword-age, shields will smash, wind-age, wolf-age, until the world falls; none shall spare another.")

It is when the wolf or dog of the apocalypse named Garmr runs free from his bonds in Gnipahellir that the world will end. That is what the poem reveals: The *vølva*, a prophetess who is reciting this poem, says that she sees ahead to the end of the world, the darkness of the gods. When Ragnarök ends—or comes—brothers will fight, siblings will destroy their bonds, and family loyalty will be gone. That is the one thing in the heathen ethos that will end the world: the loss of family.

There are two ways of spelling *Ragnarök* in Old Norse: *ragnarøkk* and *ragnarök*. The two words have different meanings and are used differently in the old stories. Ragnarøkk means "the darkness of the gods" and is used by Snorri Sturluson in his *Edda*. The other, ragnarök, is used in the old poetry, like in the poem *Vøluspá*. The last part of the word, -rök, belongs to the same root as one of the words used for the collective of the gods: *regin*.

It is also the same word as the Old Norse word for warrior and prince, *rekkr*. Ultimately, the word is related to the modern English words "regent" (ruler) and "rex" (king). The gods are rulers that have bound the world in a fated relationship. What they rule over is *ragna rök*. Another name for Óðinn is Rögnir: "ruler" or "the one who does 'ruling.'"

When the bonds that have been set by the gods are broken, and their rule in the world is being attacked by the forces of chaos, then we experience *römm sigtyva:* the darkness of the victory-gods. Such is the origin of Snorri's *ragnarøkk.* Darkness befalls the gods and the world. The *jötnar,* wardens of chaos, advance upon us and our world crumbles in flames. That is what is learned in *Vøluspá,* stanzas 47 and 52:

> *"Scelfr Yggdrasils ascr standandi, ymr iþ aldna tré, enn iötunn losnar; hrœðaz allir á helvegom, áðr Surtar þann sefi of gleypir. Surtr ferr sunnan með sviga lœvi, scínn af sverði sól valtíva; griótbiörg gnata, enn gífr rata, troða halir helveg, enn himinn klofnar."*

("The Ash-tree Yggdrasill shudders as it stands, the old tree groans, and the the *jötunn* is loose; everyone is terrified on the Hel-way, until Surtr's fire swallows them all. Surtr comes from the south with burning fire, his sword shines brighter than the sun of the death-gods; mountains crumble, trolls roam, warriors walk the way to Hel, and the sky is torn asunder.")

That is how it all ends: When the bonds are broken.

PRACTICING ÁSATRÚ TODAY

The best way to practice Ásatrú values today is to be true to yourself. This is in no way an easy task; many try to be true to themselves but have, in essence, little understanding of who they actually are. One way to figure out who you are and how you are true to yourself is to reflect upon your community: What kind of community are you part of? What does that community ask of you? Do you find yourself overextending your efforts and will to accommodate others? Always keep in mind that there needs to be balance between give and take—do not give too much and do not take too much.

CHAPTER FOUR

WORSHIP AND RITUALS

Just like every other aspect of Ásatrú, the way that heathens worship and perform rituals varies greatly depending on who they are and which groups they belong to. In this chapter, I will offer some thoughts on how to worship and perform rituals, either by yourself or as a group. Everything I describe is based on my own experiences of participating in Ásatrú rituals with groups in Denmark, Iceland, Norway, Sweden, Germany, and multiple places in the United States. Some rituals have been performed with very experienced heathens and others have been performed with newly formed groups, where the ritual may have been the first experience for most of the members present. I have held my own rituals since the middle of the 1990s. In some cases, it has been by myself; in other cases, it has been with family, friends, or a larger group of people. In the following, I will offer my insight into the different rituals and ritual practices that Ásatrúar most commonly perform. I will focus on how you can communicate with the gods, spirits, and ancestors, and how you can perform *blót*, the most common ritual in Ásatrú.

ALTAR

Not everyone has an altar, but many heathens have some kind of setup at home where they can focus their attention when they talk to the gods. An altar is made up of many different things that are meaningful to the person who made it. Do not think of an altar as something that *must* contain certain things—it can contain exactly the things you want and nothing else. An altar is a space that you build or create for yourself, composed of only the things that make you feel comfortable. I have seen heathens use two kinds of altars: indoor altars and outdoor altars.

Indoor Altars

With an indoor altar, you obviously have more options for putting things on it. If, for instance, you are a person who feels closely attached to things such as heirlooms and you want to put them on your altar, they will be more secure on your indoor altar than an outdoor one. You also have the option to put things on your indoor altar that would otherwise perish outdoors or be taken by animals.

Creating your indoor altar is rooted in how you intend to commune with the spirits. For instance, if runic meditation is something you like to do, it will be meaningful to place your set of runes on the altar. You can also place a picture, drawing, or painting of your favorite god or pictures of multiple gods. You can put rocks and plants there, too. If you like to interact with the gods and spirits through drink and food, you can have items on your altar for that. Drinking horns are very popular among Ásatrúar, especially ornately carved cow horns. You may also consider having a plate on which you put things as offerings to the gods and spirits.

Many indoor altars are focused on ancestors rather than on gods and spirits. People place pictures of their family and deceased ancestors on the altar. They hang items that used to belong to their loved ones on the altar, and in that way, the altar becomes a space in the home where you can communicate with your long-gone ancestors. Most heathens believe that the dead do not die. They live on in our memories, in our hearts, and in our surroundings. That idea is more important than any "paradise" or death-realm beyond our living world, because it means that our ancestors never abandon us.

In my house, we have a family altar, which combines the ancestors and important spirits of our combined families. We have important items on our altar, including pictures, which have belonged to our grandparents and great-grandparents. Aside from that, we have flowers and wooden carvings, ritual instruments that we use in ceremony, gifts and offerings for the gods and spirits, and many more items. All in all, what you put on your altar comes down to how you want to communicate with the gods, spirits, and ancestors.

Outdoor Altars

An outdoor altar is naturally different from an indoor one. Of course, not everyone lives somewhere that will allow for an outdoor altar, but those who do may opt for an outdoor altar. The benefit of an outdoor altar is that you can pour libations to the gods and spirits directly onto the ground. You can fashion a full space that is only to be used for ritual acts, and you can make it as beautiful as you want—for instance, as a part of your garden.

Some heathens who have the space for outdoor altars design a part of their property as a little grove with trees and sometimes a pond. Others have a large rock that they put things on for the gods and spirits. Others have an altar built of several larger and smaller rocks. Some like to mark off the area around their altar with a circle. Often, the circle is comprised of smaller rocks, wooden sticks, small fences, or rope.

While the ancient stories do not describe indoor altars, there are some that give indications of how sacred outdoor spaces were created. In the Icelandic sagas, they talk about the type of sacred sites called a *vé*. The vé is a sacred space that is marked off with *vébönd*, bonds or chains that are attached to hazelnut sticks. In several stories, there are also descriptions of special rocks and boulders, as well as ponds, lakes, and creeks, which were used as focus points for personal rituals.

Spirit-Pillars

Some heathens have *öndvégissúlur*: "spirit-way-pillars." In the saga literature, the öndvégissúlur are often mentioned in connection with the *landnám* or land-taking that the Viking settlers would perform when they came to Iceland. The standard story is that when a Viking would migrate from Norway, they would take the öndvégissúlur that they kept in their house or temple and bring them to Iceland. Once they reached Iceland, before they went ashore, they would throw the pillars overboard and let them drift to land, proclaiming that they would settle wherever the pillar washed up. The "spirit-way-pillars" were certainly important artifacts to the ancient heathens. They were conduits for communicating with the other worlds, hence the name: spirit-way-pillar.

Modern heathens often make such pillars and have them in their home, by their altar, or outside their home. The descriptions of the spirit-way-pillars are vague in the saga literature, but in the *Saga of the People of Eyri*, a man named Þórólfr Mostrarskegg is said to have had a pillar with the face of the thunder-god Þórr carved into it. The pillar also had so-called *reginna-glar*, god-nails, hammered into it. What purpose they served, the story does not say.

TALKING TO THE GODS

There are many ways that you can talk to the gods. When you talk to the gods, consider what mood you are in and why you are addressing them. There is no right or wrong way to talk to them, and you can talk to the gods as if you were praying or addressing a person. You can talk to them as if they were friends or family, even lovers or hated enemies. You can even talk to them using humor and jokes.

Heathens do not prescribe only one way that it is appropriate to talk to the gods. There are many ways, and the way you decide to address them comes down to how you feel. I have been to ceremonies where I have seen heathens talk to the gods in ways that were funny, sad, and uplifting. I have even seen heathens curse the gods, yell at them, and tell them off for all kinds of calamities that had befallen them.

Whatever you want to say to the gods, say it!

The ancient stories and poems offer some examples of how you can invoke the gods and spirits. The poem *Vøluspá* provides an example:

"Hlióðs bið ec allar helgar kindir, meiri oc minni, mögo Heimdalar; vildo, at ec, Valföðr, vel fyrtelia forn spiöll fira, þau er fremst um man."

("Listen to me, all holy beings, greater and smaller, kin of Heimdallr; Valföðr wants me to say the ancient spells, the first ones that I remember.")

The *vølva* invokes the "holy beings," who are greater and smaller, the kin of Heimdallr. Heimdallr is the god of the world; he may be the ancestor of all the living beings, so when you call upon his kin, you are addressing everyone, every god, every spirit out there. Using the formula provided by the above stanza to initiate a prayer could be a good choice. Consider modifying it to fit your personal needs. For instance:

"Listen to me, all holy beings, greater and smaller, Heimdallr's kin: I have come to ask for [state what you want]."

A recurring formula in many of the old poems is also "æsir, álfar, vissi vánir" (æsir, elves, wise vanir). This can be a good formula to end a prayer with. You can, for instance, say:

"Heilir œsir, heilir álfar, heilir vissi vánir; heil regin!"

("Hail *æsir*, hail *álfar*, hail wise *vanir*; hail *regin*.")

By doing so, you mention the primary family of the gods, the *œsir*, then the *álfar*, and then the secondary family of the gods, the *vanir*. Finally, you make sure to include all spirits by also greeting *regin*, the rulers—all of them.

An old prayer that comes from the poem *Sigrdrífomál* is Sigrdrífa's invocation before she begins to teach the young hero Sigurðr Fáfnisbani the magic of runes:

"Heill dagr, heilir dags synir, heil nótt oc nipt! Óreiðom augom lítið ocr þinig, oc gefit sitiondom sigr! Heilir æsir, heilar ásynior, heil siá in fiölnyta fold! Mál oc manvit gefit ocr mærom tveim oc læcnishendr, meðam lifom!"

("Hail day, hail the sons of day, hail night and her kin! Look on us with kind eyes and give those sitting here victory! Hail æsir, hail ásynjur, hail the bountiful earth! Give speech and wit to us two, and healing hands as long as we live.")

It is a very powerful incantation, which most certainly was used in prayer during ancient times. You can use it as a formula to create your own; change some of the words in the text with words that fit your purpose. You can take out "day" and "the sons of day" and replace them with the gods that you wish to talk to. You can use the formula as a prayer that you can say in any situation. The things that are being asked for in the prayer are universal in Ásatrú. Victory is not simply something that has to do with war—it can just as well be victory in life. Speech and wit are self-explanatory in terms of their value in Ásatrú, and healing hands are also a very valuable thing to have!

In terms of talking to the gods, my advice is simply that you find the best way that works for you. You should never worry about what is most appropriate or if you offend the gods or something in that vein: You will never offend the gods, because they are *your gods!* The gods are there for you, and you may cultivate the exact kind of relationship to them as you like. I could spend much time warning against doing or saying certain things to certain gods, but that is all based on my own personal opinion and upon my own relationship with each of them, and may not at all apply to how you want to relate to the gods. Remember this: Do not adopt the views held by others when it comes to your relationship to the gods. Discover your own.

BLÓT

The *blót*, the word for heathen rituals, is described in stanzas 144 to 145 of *Hávamál*:

> *"Veiztu, hvé rísta scal, veiztu hvé ráða scal? Veiztu hvé fá scal, veiztu hvé freista scal? Veiztu hvé biðia scal, veiztu hvé blóta scal? Veiztu hvé senda scal, veiztu hvé sóa scal? Betra er óbeiðit, enn sé ofblótið, ey sér til gildis giöf; betra er ósent, enn sé ofsóit. Svá Þundr um reist fyr þióða röc; þar hann upp um reis, er hann aptr of kom."*

("Do you know how to carve; do you know how to choose? Do you know how to color; do you know how to ask? Do you know how to invoke; do you know how to [do] blót? Do you know how to send; do you know how to slaughter? It is better not to invoke than to blót too much; a gift always requires a return; it is better not to send than to slaughter too much. Þundr carved this for the people's rule; where he raised this [stone], he returned again.")

It is a common myth that the word blót is related to the word blood, and that a *real* heathen ritual must have a blood sacrifice. There are no prescriptions for *real* heathen rituals. Therefore, blót can be what you want it to be. The origin of the word is a reconstructed proto-Germanic word *blōtá*. When scholars talk about proto-Germanic language, they are essentially talking about a language that nobody has any evidence for. It is reconstructed through the occurrence of other languages that are related to one another. So, with the proto-Germanic word *blōtá*, we have Old German, Saxon, Gothic, Old English, and Old Norse available to give us a sense of what the word comes from and might have meant long before Christianity. It is clear that the word meant "offering" and "sacrifice" in ancient times—most likely a blood sacrifice. However, it is also clear that this was not the only meaning of the word. In Old English, it also became the root of the word *blædsian*, which we know today as "blessing." In essence, blót simply means "spiritual act," or an action that we make to communicate with the gods.

Hávamál clearly suggests that there are several components of the spiritual act: carve, choose, color, ask, invoke, offer, send, slaughter. The word *sóa*, which is translated to "slaughter," refers rather to the act of partitioning an animal. In that sense, it is butchering and handing out parts of the animal to others. This is important, because it means that, traditionally, the ritual sacrifices of animals were accompanied by charitable acts and sharing. In the *Saga of Hákon the good*, there is a description of a blót ritual in which everyone had to bring cattle to the temple for slaughter, and all participants would share the meat. Adam of Bremen mentions a similar situation in his story about the temple at Uppsala in his *History of the Archbishopric of Hamburg-Bremen*. However, in it, it is the Christians in Sweden who are complaining that they have to contribute to the sacrifices.

The Forsa rune-ring is a metal ring that has been hanging on the door of a church in Hälsingland in Sweden since the Viking Age. It has a runic inscription, which seems to have been a temple law. This inscription mentions a law decree that prescribes the rates for contributions to the temples. It is clear that the ancient temple rituals, the blót that performed the large sacrifices during wintertime, existed as a way of collecting taxes and sharing food resources with the community. In the description of the Viking Rus in *Risala* from 921 CE, Ibn Fadlan records that the Viking merchants at the Volga river would go to carved idols, which represented their gods. There, they would offer them food and drink, as they asked for favors in return. If the request was honored, the Viking would return to the idols and sacrifice an animal to the gods. Ibn Fadlan writes that the Viking then gave a portion to the gods and a portion to the community as alms.

All the ancient sources suggest that *blót* was a communal event at which sharing one's resources with another was the most important part. In the ancient law of the Swedish island Gotland, it says:

"Smeri þing hafþu mindri blotan miþ fileþi, mati ok mun-gati, sum haita suþnautar, þy et þair suþu allir saman."

("Smaller assemblies had minor blót with cattle, food, and drink, and the people involved were called boiling-companions, because they would boil [food] together.")

All in all, it seems that the ancient blót rituals were communal cookouts!

Blót Today

Modern blót ritual form is primarily based on which group performs them. For instance, you can go to a blót ritual with one group and experience one version, while a few miles down the road there will be another group that does something entirely different. Some groups add as many reconstructive elements to their rituals as possible, while others do not care at all about reconstructing and simply do what they want to do. Some groups believe that blood sacrifice must be part of blót, while others have a downright ban on blood sacrifices.

One common theme of modern heathen blót rituals is that they resemble Wicca rituals. Very often, the participants gather in a circle. A goði or gyðja is in charge of leading the ritual. Some groups only have one, others have two, but there can be up to four; each of them is in charge of their part in the ritual. They will close the circle by walking around it and calling gods in each of the cardinal directions. Once they come back to their spot in the circle, they will fill a drinking horn with mead and toast to a god. The horn will go around in the circle and all the participants will do the same. It varies greatly how many times this happens and if there are other actions involved. Sometimes, there is a small fire or altar in the middle of the circle, and the participants can have personal items blessed during the ceremony.

The Goði and the Gyðja

For any kind of ritual, there should be someone leading it. It is not important how you choose a goði or gyðja, but it is important that everyone in the group feels comfortable with him, her, or them as leader(s) of the ritual. I have been goði in many blót rituals, and it is my experience that:

> If the other participants do not trust your ability to perform the role as goði, you might as well go home.

> It is always good to have at least one helper, especially if you are a large group.

> If you perform the ritual with more than one goði/gyðja, you should make sure to rehearse what you will be doing before you have the blót. That will ensure that everyone is on the same page.

As a note on the subject of choosing a goði or gyðja: I have been a member of groups in which there was a very formal structure for this, and the group would vote on who would be goði or gyðja for a certain period of time. This can work because it ensures that the person who is in charge of the ritual has the backing of at least 50 percent of the group. However, spirituality and ritual is not a democracy—it is not the same as voting for town mayor—so let us not kid ourselves. The person who ends up being a permanent leader of rituals, the goði or gyðja, in any group, is the person with:

> The most experience

> The most knowledge

> The most spiritual charisma

If you want to create a group with a goði and/or gyðja, be sure that nobody is in it to be a guru—yourself included! The world does not need any more gurus or pastors or priests or mullahs or rabbis or goðar or gyðjur who are in it to control others and gain power over vulnerable people.

If you think of yourself as a spiritual leader, look deep within yourself and ask this: Do I know how to carve, choose, color, ask, invoke, blót, send, and slaughter? If there are actions that you wish to do only for yourself, that is fine and you are welcome to do it, but if you are going to be a goði or gyðja for others, take some time to understand what stanzas 138 to 144 in *Hávamál* really mean.

Preparation

To prepare for blót, you should make it clear to yourself and anyone who is taking part in it why you are doing it. In my nearly 40 years of being part of the heathen community, I have participated in many rituals with many different people, and I have seen some curious things coming out of being unprepared and lacking communication. I fondly remember the one time I stood in a circle in the woods with a large group of people from multiple European countries. The goði had all the men in the circle chant "Óðinn," while all the women were chanting "Frigg" to a poorly executed trance-inducing beat. That memory is fond because it was a completely nonsensical experience that only humor can treat appropriately. Our goði and gyðja had a half-baked idea about how we were all going to invoke the male and female energies of Óðinn and Frigg in a shamanic trance—at 4:30 p.m., in the soggy undergrowth of a Danish forest, on a cold and gray day in April, with a bunch of strangers.

Communication and timeliness are essential to a good blót. So is place. As I mentioned before, I have been present at rituals in multiple places and countries across Europe and North America. What I have found is that blót rituals only work in places that have spirit. What does that mean? Well, it is hard to explain, but it tends to be the case that any place can, essentially, have spirit—what matters is how the spirit is treated. If you go to a place that is familiar to the goði or to several members of the group—a place where ritual has taken place several times before and at least a portion of the people there know one another—then there is a good chance of a successful blót and a positive experience for everyone.

It is also a good idea that you write down all the steps of the blót so that you do not forget something. There is nothing embarrassing about having a little manuscript for your blót, especially if you are new to the whole thing.

Items

You can bring the items that you feel you need, but most often there will be a drinking horn, because an important part of doing blót is to toast to the gods and spirits. In the old stories, it is said that a goði would carry a silver ring weighing 20 ounces. For this reason, there are many goðar and gyðjur who have such silver rings for blót—some carry them on their arm, others use them in the ritual. One way that it can be used is for holding it over the mouthpiece of the drinking horn, when mead is poured into it.

Mead is another important element for a blót. You bring mead to drink and share with the gods and spirits. The participants stand in a circle and pass around a drinking horn filled with mead. When everyone is done speaking to the gods, spirits, and ancestors, the goði will take the horn and pour out the remaining mead for the landvættir, or the spirits of the place.

If you intend to build an altar as a focal point for the circle, you should also bring the things to build it with. Some people use a table, others build an altar from stones. In the Eddic poem *Hyndluhlióð*, Freyja says that altars are built as piles of rocks. That is advice I have always followed. When I have blót, I build a rock altar around a fireplace and put the things that we use for the ritual on it.

Bring containers for the things you need that you do not intend to drink or eat yourself. For instance, I always bring a little clay cup with salt and before I begin any blót, I spit a swig of rum into the fire and pour salt for Loki. This is to make sure that he brings the offering to the rightful owners and does not take it for himself.

Some heathens also bring musical instruments, such as drums, lyres, flutes, and harps, for different parts of the ritual, but it really depends on what they feel like doing during the blót. Some also bring feathers and bundles of sage or pine or any other kind of plant that they like to use to cleanse the space.

Some people like to wear robes or reconstructed Viking Age garb. If you feel compelled to do that, go right ahead, but know that most Ásatrúar frown upon it. They feel that it waters down their spirituality and turns it into cosplay.

Invocation

Let us say that you have all decided to make a blót in the way that I usually like to do it. You have built an altar of rocks by a fire and are all standing around that fire. The goði is standing with their back turned to the north. Let us say that you have decided to also have a gyðja, who stands opposite the goði, with their back to the south. Doing so works for a smaller group, but if you are a larger group, it may be better for the goði and gyðja to stand next to each other.

What I usually do next is recite parts of *Vøluspá*:

"Hlioðs bið ec allar helgar kindir, meiri oc minni, mögo Heimdalar; vildo, at ec, Valföðr, vel fyrtelia forn spiöll fira, þau er fremst um man. Ec man iotna ár um borna, þá er forðom mic fœdda höfðo; nío man ec heima, nío ívidi, miötvið mœran fyr mold neðan. Ár vas alda þat er Ymir bygði, vara sandr né sœr né svalar unnir; iörð fannz œva né upphiminn, gap vas ginnunga, enn gras hvergi. Áðr Burs synir biöðum um yppo, þeir er miðgarð, mœran, scópo; sól scein sunnan á salar steina, þá var grund groin grœnom lauki."

("Listen to me, all holy beings, greater and lesser, kin of Heimdallr; Valföðr wants that I tell you the ancient spells, the first ones I remember. I remember *jötnar* in the early times, those who fed me in the past; I remember nine worlds, nine great women, the world tree under the earth. It was the beginning of time when Ymir lived, there was no sand, no sea, no cool waves; earth did not exist, nor heaven high up, there was a yawning void, and no grass. Until the sons of Burr lifted the ground; they created mighty middle-earth; sun shone on the stones of the hall, then the green plants grew across the ground.")

These are the first four stanzas of *Vøluspá* that describe the beginning of the world in the way that the vølva saw it. By using this part of the poem, you are setting the tone. You are reminding everyone of their origin, and you are collapsing time between *now* and *then*—the present and the time of creation. Usually, we will have the goði recite it in Old Norse and the gyðja repeat it in translation.

After we have done this, the goði and gyðja carry bundles of sage that they have lit in the holy fire, around the circle of participants. The gyðja walks from south to west, where she calls upon a chosen god or goddess; then she goes to the north and calls upon another god or goddess. Meanwhile, the goði walks to the east and calls upon a god or goddess, then he walks to the south and does the same. Both the goði and the gyðja then follow the circle back to their original spot, walking with the course of the sun. When they are done, they throw the rest of the sage or pine bundle in the fire.

After that, I give Loki his salt and rum, and I thank the gods for joining us with the formula:

"Hail *æsir*, hail *álfar*, hail *vissi vánir*!"

Offering

You should always bring an offering for performing a blót. Bring something that you will give to the gods or to a specific god, your personal gift to them. The group should also make sure to bring something that is for all the gods on behalf of the group—from community to community. The whole world is reciprocal: *Do ut des*—give to receive. You should never expect that anything comes freely to you; everything has a price.

Usually, a blót will contain a meal. The ritual circle is one part, the communal eating is another. Some choose to have the ritual after the meal, others choose to have it before. Regardless of how you may do this, make sure to always bring a plate of food for the gods, exactly like you would have prepared it for yourself.

If, on the other hand, you are sacrificing animals, this is now the time to do that. I will leave that part to your own methodolgies, but strongly underline that anyone who does so should be knowledgeable about, and compliant with, their local laws and have the appropriate permits for doing so.

Blessing

When the offering has been given, it is a good time to make blessings. Usually, nobody makes blessings of the participants unless it is a blood sacrifice. With a blood sacrifice, the blood from the slaughtered animal is used to sprinkle on the participants, or some people simply mark their hands, cheeks, or forehead with the blood from the sacrifice.

In other situations, different items that the participants have brought with them are blessed. Maybe you have a favorite item, such as a Thor's hammer pendant, or an important tool or weapon. You can bring that, put it on the altar, and have it blessed in the way that you see fit.

Sharing

Sharing is the most important part of blót. Regardless of how you decide to do blót, sharing is the one thing that you should never forget. You share food and drink with the people around you, the gods, the spirits, the land, the sky, the water, and the plants. Share your wealth like an ancient Viking chieftain. In the ancient skaldic poetry from the Viking Age, there are 438 ways of describing a generous man or a generous ruler with a kenning. There are only two other subjects that have more kennings: battle and warriors.

PRACTICING ÁSATRÚ TODAY

Remember that you do not need to belong to a group or community to be Ásatrú. You can practice on your own and do blót and other rituals all by yourself. If you choose to go out and find a group to practice with, do not stay too long if they are not to your taste. It can be a lonely feeling to be the only Ásatrúar in a place, but it is incredibly important that the ones you practice with are good, honest, and genuine people.

CHAPTER FIVE

SACRED RITUALS

All religions and spiritualities have sacred rituals, life rituals, and initiation rituals that the practitioners will participate in and celebrate at different stages in their lives. Ásatrú, however, does not have a set of specific rituals that everyone follows. As you may have realized by now, the reason for this is that heathen spirituality is non-dogmatic and community-centered. We practice our spirituality in the company of our friends and family, our kin, our *frændir*. Our spirituality is of the people and for the people, as it says in *Hávamál* 145: "*Svá Þundr um reist fyr þjóða röc.*" ("Þundr carved it so for the people's rule.")

Þundr is typically believed to be one of Óðinn's names. However, it is Óðinn in one of his more powerful roles. The name means "thunder-er," and one might think that it was another god of whom the old ones were thinking, but that is a theological discussion. The important thing to understand is that the ancient and very powerful god Þundr carved runic letters decreeing the mystical rules for the old heathen tribes: *þjóð*. There are many words for "people" in Scandinavian languages, but the ancient word þjóð is perhaps the most important one, because it signifies a coherent tribal unit that shares customs and thoughts on an intimate level.

When Þundr carved rules for rituals for *þióða röc*, the ancient god never set any universal rules, but rather, gave all tribes the capacity to create their own customs, cultures, and beliefs. It was as true then as it is now.

HEATHEN HOLIDAYS

In the following, I will give a description of some heathen holidays and seasonal rituals that you can choose to celebrate, if you like. Since heathen spirituality is not grounded in dogma, these are by no means *the real and true holidays* of heathens, because there is no such thing. Rather, I am going to describe to you what the ancient stories, the sagas, and other medieval documents suggest when it comes to historical holidays that were celebrated by heathens. I am also going to give you a broad sense of what many heathen communities seem to do, in general.

The *Blót* Cycle: Solstices and Equinoxes

It is commonly agreed among heathens that blót takes place at different times of the year. Largely, heathen groups across the world agree that there should be a blót in the spring, summer, fall, and winter, but that is the extent of the agreement. Some groups celebrate only the four holidays, while others celebrate many more.

Ásatrú groups often set the four yearly blót according to the solstices and equinoxes. The winter solstice marks the *jólablót* (yule), the spring equinox marks the *várblót*, the summer solstice marks *miðsumarr* (midsummer), and the fall equinox marks the *haustblót*. Usually, heathen groups will find a weekend around the time of the solstices and equinoxes to gather and have a blót ritual.

The ritual calendar for blót has been adopted under influence from Wicca's rendition of a mix of Celtic and Germanic holidays. Wicca and witchcraft groups see the calendar as a "year wheel," which usually has eight holidays: Imbolc (February), Ostara (March—spring equinox),

Beltane (April/May), Midsummer (June—summer solstice; also sometimes called Litha), Lughnasadh (August), Mabon/Autumn (September—fall equinox), Samhain/Halloween (October), and Yule (December—winter solstice). As a result of the mingling of Ásatrú and Wicca in the 1970s to 1980s, it is common for modern heathens to follow a holiday calendar that is, at best, an offshoot of Wicca's calendar. In many ways, the Wiccan calendar and its modern Ásatrú versions are easily and neatly applicable for life in modern times, and this makes them convenient and useful if you are new to Ásatrú.

In recent years, several heathen groups in both Europe and North America have attempted to reconstruct the ancient calendars of northern Europe. The calendars seem to have been very different from the straightforward Wiccan calendar. Remember that, even if the Wiccan calendars and the modern Ásatrú offshoots are not historically correct, they are still based on historical facts from ancient texts. This, however, does not make them accurate, and heathens who look for accuracy have turned to scholars of pre-Christian Scandinavian religion.

There are several scholarly suggestions regarding what a pre-Christian Nordic calendar may have looked like but *do not be fooled!* None of them can be verified as true—*they are all our best suggestion!* The most recent and relatively popular calendar is one presented by the Swedish scholar Andreas Nordberg in his dissertation from 2006: *Jul, disting och förkyrklig tideräkning.* The book is only available in Swedish, so most American heathens have come to know its content from Scandinavians.

Nordberg suggests that ancient Scandinavians used a calendar that followed a three-year cycle, a nine-year cycle, and a 19-year cycle similar to the Metonic calendar known from ancient Greece, which ultimately had its origins in ancient Babylon. Considering that all of Europe learned farming from that area, it would not be surprising if they also picked up early calendars from the Golden Crescent, as calendars and agriculture are intricately linked.

The older calendars are so-called lunisolar calendars, where the months follow the moon's cycle (hence the word *month*), but in order to account for the discrepancy between the moon's phases and the solar year, every third year has an extra month. The difference between the lunar and solar year is 11 days, which adds up to a full lunar month occurring in the third year. In fact, if you were to look at ancient Germanic calendars, you would find that several of them have a 13th month incorporated within them.

In order to figure out time-reckoning within the complicated lunisolar system, the winter solstice was used as the anchor for the lunar months. It is a common misconception that yule or *jól* used to be celebrated on the winter solstice in December. Instead, Nordberg suggests that the *jólablót* took place on the first full moon after the solstice, and that it would mark the new year, *hökunótt*. In short, this means that jól would actually fall on any given date in the interval between January 5 and February 2, when the new full moon after the solstice occurred. All other months and holidays in the forthcoming year would then be placed in accordance with the first full moon occurring between January 5 and February 2.

If this is true—and I think there is reason to believe it—it means that very few modern heathens are actually following the traditional calendar. Instead, they are following a calendar that was invented in the early 20th century for another neo-pagan belief system, although based on old and possibly pre-Christian calendars from Western Europe. I will leave it to you to make up your own mind about the subject and proceed to describe the different holidays that are mentioned in the old stories from Scandinavia.

Dísþing/Dísablót, Vár, Gói: Spring Celebrations

Every culture has celebrated the spring, and the pre-Christian cultures of Northern Europe are no exception. In Scandinavia, the spring celebration has historically been referred to by a variety of names. *Dísþing* is an old word for a celebration that would take place in the period around April-May. The word means "Assembly of the *dísir*" and was in use in Sweden as late as the 1700s, where local peasants would count *aunings* until the next dísþing. It is clear that this tradition of counting aunings comes from pre-Christian times, because the word is derived from an ancient pre-Christian god-king named Aun, who according to legend ruled in Uppsala. In the Icelandic sagas, however, the *Dísablót* is said to take place in the fall, which is most likely a mistake on behalf of the Icelandic tradition.

The dísþing tradition comes together with an ancient Scandinavian tradition of having spring markets near wells, streams, and bodies of water, which was also practiced in ancient Ireland, England, and Wales. Since the word has something to do with the *dísir*, it is natural for many heathens to celebrate the goddesses in the springtime.

Snorri Sturluson mentions two goddesses in his *Edda*: Vár ("oath") and Vör ("aware"). Neither has anything to do with spring. However, modern Scandinavians, except Icelanders and the Faroese, cannot distinguish the names from the modern Nordic word for "spring," *vår*, so in modern Scandinavian Ásatrú, there is a goddess named Vár or Vår, who is the goddess of spring. The modern Scandinavian word for spring is based on a now-lost Old Nordic and Old Norse word, which was spelled *vár* (like the word for "oath") and meant "spring," so it is not impossible that there once was a goddess named Vár, whose name meant "spring." Unfortunately, she is not documented.

The only possible goddess for the spring that can be identified in the ancient Scandinavian stories is Gói. According to the *Saga of the Orkney Earls*, Gói was daughter of the eponymous figure Nór, the founder of Norway. Nór descended from Þorri, who descended from Snjór (snow), who descended from Frosti (frost), who was the son of Kári (wind). Kári was the son of Fornjótr, an ancient *jötunn*, who was possibly identical to the primordial being Ymir. Gói is the name of an old Icelandic winter month from the middle of February to the middle of March, and the meaning of her ancestors' names suggests that behind this legendary genealogy, there is an ancient myth about the calendar and a possible spring goddess named Gói.

In Anglo-Saxon and continental Germanic heathenry or Ásatrú, the goddess Ēostre or Ôstara is often celebrated as a spring goddess. This goddess's name comes from the Old English historian Bede's *The Reckoning of Time*. Bede mentions *eastur-mōnath* or Easter Month. In Old High German, there is a similar name for Easter, namely Ôstarûn. In *Teutonic Mythology*, Jacob Grimm suggested that the English and German word for Easter was derived from the name of an ancient Germanic goddess, and there is no reason to doubt that. A common misconception is that the goddess is the same as the Mesopotamian goddess Ishtar. That is not the case. Etymologically, Ēostre or Ôstara is associated with the goddess known in Old Indian (Vedic) as Ušas, in Greek as Eos, in Roman as Aurora, and in Lithuanian as Aušra, and it seems that she may have been the goddess of the spring and of the dawn. The ritual that was performed during the celebration of Ēostre may have something to do with the Anglo-Saxon poem *œcerbot*, the field remedy charm.

It is possible that Ēostre/Ôstara was known in Scandinavia. Although the Scandinavians lost their own word for spring celebrations and adopted the church-Latin Pascua—*påske*—the peoples on the Jutland peninsula in Denmark have traditionally celebrated the *Osterfeuer* (Easter Fire) like their cousins in the Netherlands, Niedersachsen, Hessen, Frisia, and elsewhere in northwestern Germany. The tradition of lighting a wheel on fire and celebrating the sun is believed to be an ancient custom associated with the spring goddess.

Miðsumarr and *Fagna Sumri*: Summer Celebrations

There are no sources to authenticate an ancient midsummer tradition. In the Icelandic sagas, there is sometimes the mention of *fagna sumri*, "rejoice in summer," which some believe was a ritual. From it also stems the vague reference to *sigrblót*, a ritual that Vikings would have for victory before they traveled abroad. None of the mentions are particularly credible or well-described, but, nonetheless, they are not completely unacceptable as historical practices.

Many modern heathens celebrate Midsummer on the summer solstice. Usually, the celebration includes the Midsummer Pole, which is also sometimes called a May Pole. The *midsommarstång*, as the Midsummer Pole is called in Swedish, is an old Scandinavian folk-custom, which migrated there from Germany in the 1500s. Originally, the Midsummer Pole represented the Christian cross, but in Ásatrú tradition, it has come to symbolize the world tree, Yggdrasill or Îrminsûl.

Haustr, Vetrnœtur, and *Fagna Vetri*: Fall Celebrations

Another poorly described ritual in the sagas is *fagna vetri*, the celebration of winter. The fall is also referred to as *høst* in modern Danish and Norwegian, *höst* in modern Swedish, and therefore known as *haustr* in Old Norse. That the ancient Scandinavians had rituals for *haustr* is self-evident—again, that is something that is so universal that, even if it is not described in the old stories, it must have taken place, just like it did after conversion. This celebration seems to have taken place in the end of the summer, probably in the middle or end of August.

Vetrnœtur is a ritual that is also very sparsely described. It means "winter nights" and it is called that because it takes place at the end of fall, marking the transition to winter. It is typically conflated with *fagna vetri* in the sagas. Many modern heathens consider the winter nights to be the same as the Anglo-Saxon *modraniht*, "mothers' night," and perhaps Halloween. Some consider this ritual to be the same as *dísablót* and *álfablót*, another ritual that seems to have taken place in the wintertime. Mostly, heathens treat these rituals as ancestral rituals, where you honor the ancestors in some way. Some also treat them as exclusively goddess-focused rituals.

Jól: Winter Celebrations

Jól or yule, the precursor to Christmas, is of course the most well-described ritual in all of the old stories that are available today. In the *Saga of Hákon the good*, the ritual is described as a large communal sacrifice that took place in a temple at Møre in central-northern Norway. People would sacrifice animals, cook them, and eat them.

The description of the ritual at Møre pits the Christian king, Hákon, against some stubborn heathen subjects of his. As the king, Hákon is expected to participate in the ritual, but he does not want to. When it is time to eat the horse meat that has been prepared, Hákon puts a piece of cloth over it when he bites down. Similarly, he makes the sign of the cross over the drinking horn before he is about to drink the mead. One of the participants asks Hákon's helpful earl what the king is doing, and the earl replies that Hákon made the sign of "Thor's hammer" over the drinking horn. This passage has led modern heathens to consider horse meat particularly important for blót, especially at *jólablót*. Many heathen groups in Scandinavia eat horse meat at the blót, and making the so-called "hammer sign" has become a common thing to do among heathens in North America, even though in the saga it is clearly a joke.

As a modern heathen holiday, *jól* is certainly the biggest one. It is described in the ancient stories in different ways, which has prompted heathens and non-heathens in Scandinavia to assume that *jól* was in existence before Christianity. While that may be, it is important to understand that any modern traditions that Scandinavians and non-Scandinavians have today are not survivals of ancient heathens.

Modern heathens have picked up on folk-customs from Scandinavia and northern Europe, which have been in existence for a very long time but cannot be authenticated as ancient heathen customs. The *julebukk*, a straw goat that is used for decorations, is a good example of that. In Scandinavia, it was also a custom until the beginning of the 20th century to dress up as a goat instead of Santa and hand out gifts. Some heathens believe Santa is really Óðinn, who has been "Christianized" over the centuries, but that is incorrect. Another incorrect assumption is that the Christmas tree has something to do with ancient pre-Christian traditions. There is nothing that can support that idea; in fact, we know that the Christmas tree became widely used in the late 19th century and early 20th century, not before, with the tradition originating in Germany. In Scandinavia, it was customary to decorate the inside of the house with pine before the German Christmas tree tradition: People would cut pine branches and leave them lying around all over the house. However, the tradition does not reach all the way back to heathen times.

In the sagas, it is said that you "drink *jól*" and brew beer for the event. There is also an instance of swearing oaths by placing your hand on the back of a hog. This suggests that eating pork and drinking beer is an important part of *jól*. Scandinavian heathens, and especially Danes and Swedes, have cultivated this tradition, because beer and pork are already common on the Christmas table and have been since the late 19th century.

Many modern heathens have adopted customs and traditions that do not come from the pre-Christian customs but were invented in the span of the last 500 years and there is absolutely nothing wrong with that: The heathen tradition is non-dogmatic and evolves over time. If it makes sense for you to use traditions that have recently been invented, go right ahead. One could make the argument that this is exactly what heathenry is all about: a constant reinvention and repurposing of tradition in a way that makes sense in modern times. What does not make sense, however, are the claims in books and on the internet about recent Christian traditions being ancient heathen traditions. Do not fall for such claims—those who make the claims typically want to push a modern heathen dogma about *how things really are* in order to claim their personal right to traditions and take them away from others. Steer clear of that.

Þórshelgi

A great example of a modern heathen invention that has been created on the backbone of Christian traditions in Scandinavia is *þórshelgi* or *thorshelg*. This is a Swedish tradition, which has its roots in the Västergötland area around Gothenburg. The local group of Ásatrúar there have invented a tradition where they celebrate every Thursday (Thor's Day) for six weeks before the winter solstice. They light candles with runes written on them and say a runic prayer for each one. This is called *väntljusstaken* (waiting-candleholder) and it is a good way for heathen Scandinavian parents to provide the same tradition for their children as the Christian advent tradition. In Scandinavia, the advent tradition is very important, and children usually get gifts from the parents on each Sunday in advent before Christmas Eve. By inventing the *thorshelg* and *väntljusstake*, this heathen community in Sweden has successfully done the most heathen thing you can do: They have made sure that they and their children can participate in society on equal terms with everyone else, instead of separating themselves from society based on religious inclination.

This is what being heathen is all about. Do you recall the Icelandic law-speaker who decreed that Iceland should have Christian law, because although he was a heathen, he was more concerned with keeping society together than tearing it apart over religious differences? In the same way, the Northern tradition has adapted and changed with time and societal developments. Scandinavians may have converted to Christianity and established Christian countries in old heathen lands, but the heathens are still there—they exist because the Norse gods were able to live on in new forms, and now there are heathens creating modern heathen traditions in the 21st century.

LIFE RITUALS

Except for funeral rituals, there are very few direct descriptions of life rituals in the old stories from the medieval period. Little is known regarding life events celebrated by ancient heathens. As a result, modern heathens are left to their own creativity.

Birth

Every Ásatrú group and family has unique birth rituals. There is not a uniform ancient custom to refer to in modern times. However, an ancient tradition is the *nornagraut*, the *norns'* porridge. The goddesses of fate called the *nornir* are responsible for setting the fate of a human with fate-threads when they are born. This is beautifully described in the heroic Eddic poem *Helgaqviða hundingsbana in fyrri*, in stanza 3:

> *"Snero þær af afli ørlögþátto, þá er borgir braut í Brálundi; þær um greiddo gullin símo oc und mána sal miðian festo."*

("They [the *nornir*] turned powerfully the strings of fate, when burrows shook in Brálund [on Earth]; they tangled the golden threads and set them in the middle of the Moon's Hall [the sky].")

To give the *nornir* thanks for setting a good fate for the newborn, it was an old custom (in the Faroe Islands, Denmark, and Setesdal in Norway) for the woman who had given birth to share *nornagraut* with the *nornir*.

People would prepare a special porridge and the woman would share it with her married female friends, including a portion that was given to the *nornir*. The tradition also existed among the Sámi, who would prepare Sárakka-porridge for the goddess Sárakka. Both in the Sámi tradition and in the Danish tradition, people would place three sticks in the porridge. In the Sámi tradition, one stick would be white, one would be black, and the third one would have three rings carved on it. The sticks would be put under the threshold of the door before nightfall, and they would tell the fortune of the mother and child based on which of the sticks had been taken during the night. There is no similar information about the Danish custom with the sticks, except that they seem to have represented the three *nornir*: Urðr, Verðandi, and Skuld.

In the Faroese and Danish traditions, there is also the idea of *nornaspor*. If a child has a white spot on its nail, it is a *nornaspor* (*norn's* mark), and it tells the fortune of the child. This has a counterpart in the Eddic poem *Sigrdrífomál*, where stanza 7 says that power-runes should be carved on the drinking horn, the back of your hand, and—to gain power-runes—you should mark your nail with *nauð*, the n-rune: n. The n-rune has been used in magic formulas since the earliest times. In an old Anglo-Saxon charm for healing, from the 11th century, it says, *"Neogone wæran Noþðæs sweoster"* ("They were nine, Nauð's sisters"). This seems to be another reference to *nornir*—here including the magical number nine, too. It is clear that the *nornir* were considered healing powers and traditionally were believed to have a hand in birth.

Naming

The old heathen way of naming a child is referred to as *knésetja*, placing a child on the knee. It would occur at the assembly, the *þing*, when the child was three years old, and not before. In the time before the child was named, it could in principle be abandoned without legal consequences. Doing so was the old Scandinavian way of "abortion." Children would be left in the marsh, the forest, or to be taken by the ocean, especially if there was no way to feed them or if they were ill. However, doing so was not legal after the child had been given a name. At the assembly, the father would place the child on his knee and proclaim the child's name and lineage. Many modern heathen families continue that part of the tradition: gathering with friends and family or bringing their child to the local or national gathering of their group and having a knee-setting ceremony.

Coming of Age

There are no historical descriptions of rituals for coming of age, for any gender. As a result, modern heathens have developed their own rituals. In Scandinavia, the Christian ritual of confirmation is very popular in society in general. This means that non-Christians tend to also have a celebration at that same time in life, when one turns 13 or 14. Muslims, Jews, Buddhists, atheists, and heathens alike in Denmark, Norway, Sweden, and Iceland often celebrate *non-firmation* instead of confirmation. As a teenager, my parents held such a celebration for me, for which we had a ritual that was focused on instructing me in what it meant to be an adult. That is the important part: becoming an adult. I received gifts: Mostly, I was given money by friends and family, but my parents also gave me a little Thor's hammer pendant on a chain and a copy of the Eddic poems. Other families have more elaborate rituals, and some have more minimalistic rituals.

Marriage

There are no descriptions of ancient heathen weddings in the old stories. What is known is that they probably took place at the assembly, where a marriage would be declared between two parties. Moreover, the Icelandic sagas typically describe the situations as the man, seeking to marry a woman, basically makes an arranged marriage with the father of the woman. While some may think that it is romantic for a man to ask the father of his future bride for permission to marry her, doing so is not what people did in ancient Scandinavia. It very much seems like marriage was more a political alliance than a romantic action. The only hint of a wedding ceremony is the story about Þórr who loses his hammer to Þrymr in the Eddic poem *Þrymsqviða*. Þórr is forced to dress up as Freyja and go to Þrymheimr and marry the *jötunn*. When the ceremony is about to begin, they take the hammer out to put it in the bride's lap as some form of blessing. Scholars and heathens alike have made a lot out of that information, but it is unclear what it actually represented.

In modern Scandinavia, the national Ásatrú organizations are licensed to perform legal weddings. Whether it is in Iceland, Norway, Denmark, or Sweden, organizations have professional goðar and gyðjur who can help you plan a wedding exactly how you like it. In Iceland, the national organization, Ásatrúarfélagið, has performed many weddings for American heathens and has traditionally been very open to doing that for Americans—especially same-sex couples. All the Scandinavian Ásatrú organizations are very open and welcoming to same-sex couples. It is also the case for the large American organization, the Troth.

Funeral

There are several historical sources pertaining to funeral rites. Ibn Fadlan's description of the funeral ritual that took place in Russia in 921 CE is one of the good ones. Aside from that, there are plenty of archaeological sites that suggest various ritual practices. Of course, many of the elements in ancient Viking funeral rites are not appropriate today, especially the animal sacrifices (not to mention human sacrifices), so if you want to reconstruct anything from then, you should consider one thing: How can your modern life be reflected in a similar way—not the same way—as was the custom back then? Grave goods were a very common thing in ancient Viking funerary rites, as was cremation. Usually, people cremated the dead and raised a rune stone or another kind of monument in their memory. Ancient practices such as cremation can easily be adapted to modern times, where you can legally be cremated with small items, such as prized possessions, in the coffin.

PRACTICING ÁSATRÚ TODAY

Heathens often say that Ásatrú is a spirituality with homework: If you want to be a modern heathen, you find yourself in need of being creative. Nothing will come to you and tell you what to do. This can be both good and bad. It can be good because you have the freedom to be your own person and explore your own way of being heathen; it can be bad because you can find yourself without direction. For rituals, find yourself a tight-knit group of friends and family to practice with. It does not matter if all of you are new to it; you can explore the best ways of creating modern heathen rituals together. Doing so will most certainly be a very rewarding experience for everyone!

CHAPTER SIX

MAGIC AND ESOTERIC PRACTICES

Some heathens are very determined to distinguish the magical practices of Ásatrú from the *magick* of Wicca and witchcraft because some modern heathens see post-conversion practices as corrupted by Christianity. In this chapter, I will explain how modern heathens use magic and esoteric practices in their daily lives, with focus on the ongoing discussion of *when* and *where* to draw the line in *what can be defined as truly heathen.* Recall that heathenism is a worldview, which means that there is no dogma—and where there is no dogma, there is no need for "pure" scripture or practice.

GERMANIC MAGIC

Germanic magic is a term that heathens sometimes use, while others use "Scandinavian magic," "Norse magic," or the Nordic words *trolldom/trolddom/fjölkynngi/galdra/galder*. From a scholarly point of view, there is nothing that distinguishes "Germanic" magic from types practiced in other ethnic groups throughout Europe and in other places across the world. Germanic magic is fundamentally similar to Sámi and Finnish/Baltic magic, Slavic magic, Roman, Greek, Spanish, Romanian, Greenlandic Inuit magic, and so on. The basis for magic is the idea that you can manipulate the world around you by interacting with spirits. In that sense, scholars also point out that modern Christians practice magic through prayer: When you pray and ask God for something, you are essentially trying to cause changes in the world by appealing to a spirit.

Historically, the idea that you can change the world by appealing to spirits has been a problem to Christianity, because magic essentially means that—from the Christian perspective—you are changing God's creation. For all of northern Europe, and especially Scandinavia, the Anglo-Saxon abbot, Ælfric of Eynsham (circa 955 to 1020 CE), became important for defining what was *magic* and *esoteric arts*. Ælfric wrote the homily *The False Gods*, which was used by the archbishop of York and later translated into Norse. According to Ælfric there are two kinds of magic: black magic and white magic. Black magic is where you take your appeal to the agents of Satan, whereas white magic is, in essence, when you perform divination and are guided by God. Obviously, the traditional forms of magic in northern Europe—all the kinds of magic that had something to do with appealing to the old gods—were considered black magic, because the old gods were agents of the devil: demons!

Indigenous magic always functions on the same terms, whether it is in northern Europe or elsewhere. You appeal to gods and spirits by giving them gifts; you divine the future or a person's intentions by using ritual instruments that connect you with a god or spirit; you get possessed by a god or spirit; your spirit travels to another realm through transcendental shamanic rituals. Such rituals remain fairly common in cultures across the world, and they were fundamental to religious practices in northern

Europe before and after conversion to Christianity—it is, in fact, only within the last 200 to 300 years that they have waned significantly in European culture. Today, the average person probably knows of these kinds of rituals from exaggerated examples in horror movies like *The Exorcist* or *The Witch*. If you were to go back some 400 years, most people would be familiar with some variation of them.

In what is often called Germanic magic, there are at least five ways to connect with the gods and spirits. The most popular modern way to do so is by working with runes. Some also perform *galdr*, which in the old stories is a form of song magic. The third kind of magic is *gandr*, staff-magic, and it is often connected with *galdr*. *Seiðr* is the most popular kind of magic aside from rune working. There are many *vǫlur*, female ritual specialists, who practice *seiðr*. *Útiseta* is a form of meditative practice or chanting practice that is often used in *seiðr*. Let's take a few moments to look at how the various forms of magic are practiced during modern times, but before that, I will need to explain the terms for such magic-workers, which are known from the old stories: *vǫlva* and *þulr*.

THE *VǪLVA* AND THE *ÞULR*

In the old stories, the term *vǫlva* (plural: *vǫlur*) is often used as the term for a female ritual specialist: someone who is in charge of rituals. The word is derived from the Norse word *vǫlr*, which means "staff." This word is derived from proto-Germanic *waluz* and is cognate with the Latin *vallus*, "stake." In his *Germania* from 98 CE, Tacitus talks of a "witch" who led the Germanic tribe, the Bructeri, in a rebellion against the Romans. Her name was Weleda and it is possible that her name comes from the same origin as *vǫlr* and *vǫlva* in that proto-Germanic word *waluz*. If that is true, the *vǫlva* is the oldest identifiable religious authority in northern European culture.

The best known Eddic poem, *Vǫluspá*, is the prophecy of a *vǫlva*. In the poem, the *vǫlva* remembers the creation of the world and sees its destruction. She is cast as the most ancient "human" figure, older than the creation of humans themselves. In the *Saga of Eirikr the Red*, a *vǫlva* performs a divination ritual, where she sits on a *stallr*, a pedestal or altar, and goes into a shamanic trance while the other women present chant a *varðlokkur* song. In the sagas, the vølva is sometimes mentioned with great respect, while in other cases she is treated as a horrible witch. It is most likely that the cases in which she is called a witch reflect the Christian authors' attitudes. In Ibn Fadlan's description of the Viking chieftain's burial in Russia, there is an "Angel of Death" who is in charge of the sacrifices and all the ritual elements—it is possible that this was in fact a vølva.

Where the vølva is often mentioned in Norse literature, the *þulr* is much more mysterious. The earliest appearance of the word is on the 9th century Snoldelev rune-stone in Snoldelev, just south of Copenhagen in Denmark. In place-names, it is also known from Tulehøj ("þulr-mound"), the previous name for the Copenhagen suburb Frederiksberg in Denmark. In poetry, the word appears earliest in *Beowulf*, in the Old English form *þyle*, and later in Eddic poetry from Iceland. In *Hávamál*, Óðinn is called *Fimbulþulr*: The great þulr, and stanza 111 begins with:

"Mál er at þylja, þular stoli á, Urðarbrunnr at . . ."

("It is time to recite from the reciter's throne at the well of Urðr . . .")

In Norse *at þula* seems to have meant "to speak," and a þulr would have been a reciter. In Old English, *þyle* meant "orator" and *þylcræft* meant "elocution." A þulr was in ancient times a poet, a speaker of sorts, perhaps the precursor to the skalds, and most certainly a ritual specialist or "priest" under the guidance of Óðinn in his role as *Fimbulþulr*. In the Eddic poem *Rigsþula*, the god Rig (King) teaches the youngling *Konr ungr* (a name that also means "king," but specifically in the sense of hereditary kingship) the language of birds and, naturally, the secret of the runes.

RUNES

It is clear that runes have historically had an important role in magic, and that, in the earliest times, using runes was associated with the warriors and aristocracy. In *Rigsþula*, Konr ungr was initiated into a cult of Óðinn in order to learn and understand the runes and other esoteric secrets.

Undoubtedly, this was an important part of preparing the upper class, the rulers and ritual specialists in the ancient times. The nornir also write with runes in *Vøluspá* and *Sigrdrífumál*, so there is reason to believe that the vølur and other female ritual specialists, or aristocratic women, would also have needed to know runes.

The first runes appear on the Viemose inscription from the Danish island Fyn around 150 CE. They were probably in use before then and Tacitus mentions that the Germanic peoples use *notae* to divine the future. The Latin word *notae* means "inscriptions," so it is possible that he was referring to runes. To know how to read runes was a mark of distinction in the Migration Age and into the Viking Age, but with the emergence of the rune-stone trend during the Viking Age, it seems that knowledge of runes became increasingly common.

Rune-stones are monuments raised by elites in Scandinavia. The tradition was not invented in the Viking Age; it began before then. During the 500s CE, specific ritual inscriptions and reference to an idea of an aristocratic priesthood of sorts begin to appear, known as *erilaz*-inscriptions. Some of them appear on rune-stones, others on objects. Usually, they refer to a man by his name and then the title *erilaz*, like the Kragehul spear from Denmark:

"Ek erilaz ānsugīsalas muha haitē ..."

("I [am] *erilaz*, son of Ānsu-gīsal, my name is Muha . . .")

The inscription suggests that Muha, son of god-hostage (a *þulr*?), called himself an *erilaz*. The word has its origin in the tribe known as the Heruli, who migrated back to Scandinavia from the Austrian-Hungarian area just prior to 500 CE, when their kingdom was destroyed. They brought their tribal name with them back to Scandinavia, and it seems that the name then became the title *erilaz*, which turned into earl and jarl in Old English and Norse. They were the first early rulers in Scandinavia—and possibly in northwestern Germany, the Netherlands, and Anglo-Saxon Britain—and they knew runes.

In the Viking Age, the runic inscriptions seem to become more and more mundane. The ones on rune-stones are mostly memorials to deceased family members, friends, and such. There is very little magical use of runes in the Viking Age, but after conversion, the magical use of runes reappears. This is also the time when the rune poems are composed—poems that were created to memorize the runes, but the individual stanzas about the runes seem to carry more information than simply a memory list. There is a Norwegian, an Icelandic, a Swedish, and an Old English rune poem.

After the conversion to Christianity, rune magic becomes very mixed with Christian-Jewish magic. Numerology, astrology, and Kabbalism, even Hermetic and Arabic mysticism, are mixed in with traditional rune magic. This is especially the case in the currently very popular early modern Icelandic sigil tradition, where different magical symbols such as the *vegvísir* and *œgishjálmur* have become widely known. Although aesthetically pleasing and rather cool symbols, these have their root in early Salomonic magic and generally derive from Christian-Jewish mysticism.

You can find a lot of information about runes and how to do rune magic in books and on the internet. Speaking as a scholar and heathen, so far, there is nothing available in a generally accessible form that is based on traditions that are older than the 18th century. What is even worse is that most of the rune magic you find in popular books is based on *Ariosophy*, a pseudo-scientific white supremacist ideology from the late 19th century. Such practices as rune meditation, rune yoga, and rune reading kits that include the "blank rune" and *Armanen* runes are all based on that very young tradition, which was invented by, well, white supremacists. All that has absolutely nothing to do with what the ancestors once did in terms of magic.

I cannot reveal to you what rune magic is in any broad terms besides providing you with a historical overview. This is not because I do not want to, but because rune magic is something that will become revealed to you once you start doing it yourself. You can choose to learn from someone who has practiced it for years, but you can also start out on your own. The more you immerse yourself in the study of runes, the more you will learn and understand.

What you will usually learn when you pick up a book on runes (whether it is scholarly or spirituality-based) is that there are two kinds of runes: the elder and the younger Futhark. Futhark is the name for the runic writing system, derived from the first six letters: f, u, þ (th), a, r, k. The elder futhark is known from inscriptions on stone, bone, metal, and wood from the period 150 to 700 CE. It is also often called the 24-Futhark because it had 24 letters. In the 700s, something curious happens: The Futhark is reformed in the Danish area, and the younger futhark, also known as the 16-Futhark, appears. What happens is that the Futhark is revised and eight letters from the elder Futhark are abandoned in favor of only 16 letters. Scholars are still perplexed by this, because it does not appear to be a particularly good idea, since the reduced letter system did not support all the phonetic values of the Scandinavian languages. With the younger 16-letter Futhark, all of a sudden, Scandinavians had to use the same letters for certain sounds, for instance t and d, g and k, p and b. The result is that sometimes Viking Age runes are difficult to read.

While you will find that people talk about the two Futharks, the elder and the younger, there are in fact many more. Some will also have heard of the Anglo-Saxon Futhorc—named so from the first six letters in the Anglo-Saxon runic writing system. It was used in England and in the Netherlands far into the medieval period. However, neither the Anglo-Saxon Futhorc nor the elder and younger Futharks are in fact uniform. There are different regional versions and there are also different versions in different periods. For example, there are nine different versions of the Anglo-Saxon Futhorc, and most of them are not found in the British Isles, but in the Rhineland area and Bavaria. This, of course, raises the question: Is the Anglo-Saxon Futhorc more Anglo-Saxon than German? I will let you decide that on your own.

Other important realizations include:

> There are variations in the elder Futhark.

> There are variations in the younger Futhark.

> The younger Futhark evolved again in the 1100s, when Scandinavians seemed to realize that a 16-letter writing system did not work that well for their languages.

During the medieval period, Scandinavians reintroduced letters to the younger Futhark, and regional versions began cropping up. At that point, runes became such a common thing that everyone seemed to be able to write with them. From the period 1200 to 1400, archaeologists have found thousands of little slips of bark, wood, or bone with runes on them in Bergen in Norway. The writing appears to have been made by common people who were sending everyday messages to one another. From the 1300s, runes were also being used as a regular writing system, similar to the Latin alphabet, in books such as the famous Danish *Codex Runicus* from 1300 CE, which also contains the oldest Scandinavian song. Runes were normal writing letters in the medieval period, and, in fact, some communities in Scandinavia kept using runes up to the first half of the 20th century. In many ways, runes are still being used in Scandinavia today.

Historically, there was never a central authority to control the letters, and therefore there is no real "right" or "wrong" method to how they are used, both as writing symbols and as magical symbols. There are some standards that experts in runology can see were common in the different periods, and if you wish to adhere to the standards of a certain period, I suggest that you study the runes thoroughly. Opposite is a chart of the elder and younger Futhark in their standardized forms.

The Elder and Younger Futhark

LATIN LETTERS	ELDER FUTHARK	NAMES IN PROTO-GERMANIC	MEANING	LATIN LETTERS	YOUNGER FUTHARK	NAMES IN OLD NORSE	MEANING
F	ᚠ	*fehu	Wealth	F	ᚠ	Fé	Wealth
U	ᚢ	*ūruz	Aurochs	U	ᚢ	Úr	Drizzle
TH(þ)	þ	*þurisaz	Ogre	TH(þ)	þ	Þurs	Ogre
A	ᚨ	*ansuz	God	Ā	ᚬ	Óss, Áss	God
R	ᚱ	*raidō	Journey	R	ᚱ	Reið	Ride
K	‹	*kaunan	Wound	K	ᚴ	Kaun	Wound
G	ᚷ	*gebō	Gift	H	ᚼ	Hagall	Hail
W	ᚹ	*wunjō	Joy	N	ᚾ	Nauð	Need
H	ᚺ	*haglaz	Hail	I	ᛁ	Ís	Ice
N	ᚾ	*naudiz	Need	A	ᛆ	Ár	Year
I	ᛁ	*īsan	Ice	S	ᛋ	Sól	Sun
J	ᛃ	*jēran	Year	T	ᛏ	Týr	Týr (god)
Æ/Ë/Ï	ᛇ	*īwaz	Yew tree	B	ᛒ	Bjarkan	Birch
P	ᛈ	*perþō	Choice	M	ᛘ	Maðr	Man
Ž/Dental R	ᛉ	*algiz	Elk	L	ᛚ	Lögr	Water
S	ᛊ	*sōwilō	Sun	Dental R	ᛦ	Ýr	Bow
T	ᛏ	*tīwaz	Týr (god)				
B	ᛒ	*berkanan	Birch				
E	ᛖ	*ehwaz	Horse				
M	ᛗ	*mannaz	Man				
L	ᛚ	*laguz	Water				
NG	◇	*ingwaz	Ing (god)				
O	ᛟ	*ōþilan	Homeland				
D	ᛗ	*dagaz	Day				

There are many theories on what the names of the different runes mean. There are also many versions of the names available, in books and on the internet, all of which causes confusion for modern heathens. I have chosen to present the correct names in reconstructed proto-Germanic and in Old Norse. The reconstructed proto-Germanic language is, as I have mentioned before, theoretical, and there are not any actual examples of it in writing. The Old Norse names, however, are attested in the rune poems, in the grammatical treatises written in medieval Iceland, and in scholarly works from Denmark, Norway, and Sweden in the period 1300 to 1800.

Bind-runes have become very popular in recent years. Bind-runes are often associated with the sigil tradition from 18th century Iceland, but the bind-runes are much older. Some of the earliest examples are from the Rök rune-stone in Sweden, from circa 800 CE. The traditional bind-runes, however, are simpler than the ones that modern heathens make.

GALDR

Galdr is chanting. There are no surviving sources to reveal what galdr was in the ancient times. In the old stories, Óðinn is the master of galdr and it is said that he can chant so that the ground and rocks open up. Modern heathens mostly use galdr in ritual, for instance at blót, where singing and chanting accompany the ritual acts.

In recent years, several heathen bands have emerged, such as Wardruna and Heilung. Wardruna is a Norwegian band that makes music based in Norse mythology, runes, and other ancient stories; Heilung makes music from the same sources. Both of the bands are purposefully making music that can be used in heathen rituals, and with them, a more official *galdr* tradition is emerging in Ásatrú and heathenism.

GANDR

Gandr essentially means "staff magic." In the old stories, there are several examples of people using staffs to perform magic or protect themselves from evil spirits. In some cases, the staff represents the conduit between upper and lower, just like the spirit-way-pillars, whereas in other cases, the staff represents a tree, a human, and a penis. The famous story of *Vølsa þáttr* (*Little-Staff Story*) provides a glimpse of an ancient fertility ritual, where a curated horse penis is being used in a *gandr* ritual.

Today, modern heathens usually use wooden staffs for "grounding." A goði or gyðja holds a staff during ritual in order to keep their connection to the earth. People also use staffs as directional tools during the ritual process, to draw ritual circles and much more.

Níðstöng

A particular kind of staff magic is the *níðstöng*. The níðstöng is a shaming and banning tool that is used in Scandinavia by heathens and non-heathens alike. It is known from the saga literature, where especially the famous Viking Egill Skallagrímsson is said to have used a níðstöng to curse the Norwegian royals Eiríkr blóðøx and his queen Gunnhildr. Egill made a staff with a horse head on it and performed certain magical rites to turn the landvættir against them.

In modern times, the níðstöng has been used all over Scandinavia in both political and artistic and heathen contexts. A recent example occurred in Iceland, where someone raised a nídstöng against the Icelandic parliament. In heathen circles, the nídstöng has traditionally been used to ban Neo-Nazis. Very few of these modern níð-poles actually carry real animal heads, horses or otherwise. Instead, people write messages, curses, runes, and bind-runes on them.

SEIÐR

Seiðr is probably the most private kind of magic that heathens practice. The magic is deeply personal and has to do with fate. Seiðr, as a word, has its origin in the proto-Germanic **saidaz*, which is cognate with Lithuanian *saitas*, "sing," and proto-Celtic **soito*, "magic," ultimately derived from a common root in Indo-European: **soi-to*, "string, rope." In Old German, the word *seito* is used in words for "string instrument" and "bow," suggesting that related words to seiðr kept the ancient meanings associated with strings. In the skaldic poem *Ragnarsdrápa* by the 9th century Icelandic skald Bragi Boddason, the word seiðr is used to mean "string." When you practice seiðr, you make charms that tie strings of fate together, just like the nornir and the gods. Modern heathens do that in many different ways, and in order to learn how that works, you should find a modern-day vǫlva to learn it from.

Útiseta

A part of the seiðr is *útiseta*, which simply means "sitting outside." You do that at night, and according to the old stories, the vǫlur would do it at cross-roads, burial mounds, or in caves. Modern heathens do útiseta wherever they think it works best. In the old stories, people would do this to commune with the trolls, but in modern times, most people do it for meditation practices and to better connect with nature.

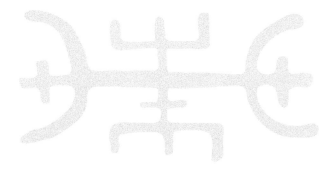

PRACTICING ÁSATRÚ TODAY

You do not have to practice magic to be heathen and you do not have to reject magic to be heathen. However you choose to view magic is ultimately your business. Many modern heathens use components of the different magical practices in their rituals because it makes sense to them. Remember that the modern distinction between ritual or ceremony and magic are artificial to our tradition—they were invented by Christian theologians, like Ælfric, who claimed that there was a difference in the way that you practice religion. Christians did that to explain and support how their own practices were deemed acceptable and right, while the "pagan" ones were not. Today, many heathens are confused by these ideas and think that the same distinctions apply, but they do not. If you want to use these magical practices, go for it!

CHAPTER SEVEN

MODERN DAY ÁSATRÚ

What role does Ásatrú have in our lives in the 21ˢᵗ century? How can you practice Ásatrú today and connect with fellow heathens in North America and throughout the rest of the world?

By now, I hope you have realized that Ásatrú in modern times *is not just one single thing*. Ásatrú is what you make of it, and you have endless possibilities for forging your relationship to the gods and spirits around you, as well as your own path in life. Many heathens say, "Ásatrú is a spirituality with homework." This is both true and not true. It is true in the sense that you do not get much of it served to you on a platter, but it is untrue in the sense that, if you do not wish to become a scholar simply to have a relationship with the gods and spirits around you, you do not really have to. When it comes to Ásatrú, it is your choice what you make of it.

Ásatrú today has evolved from a cocktail of cultural uses of an ancient tradition. People in different countries in Europe and North America, at different times, have used the Norse gods, the ancient Viking heroes, and the Germanic past in their own way. In some cases, this use has been innocent, while, in other cases, it has been part of the most unsavory kind of political schemes.

Ásatrú is still growing and evolving. It has become an ~ficial religion in many countries, known and recognized—and ~ven respected—by officials, which is a positive development, but it is important to understand that there will never be an endpoint for our development. Heathens have always evolved— *and we will always evolve.*

MYTHS AND MISCONCEPTIONS: QUESTIONS AND ANSWERS

There are many myths and misconceptions about what it means to be Ásatrú and heathen. In the following pages, I have collected some of the most common misconceptions that have come to the surface over the years.

Is Ásatrú a Spirituality of the Blood?

The idea that Ásatrú is a spirituality of the blood comes from Folkish Ásatrú. There is a small subset of heathens out there, who, like any other fundamentalist group in any other religion, believe that there are strict rules for who can be called heathen and Ásatrú. The Folkish heathens purport that you must have European blood in your veins, and that a group of heathens must share blood in different ways (either metaphorically or as a blood-brotherhood) to be "real." The bottom line is that that is utter nonsense. There is nothing in either the historical records or in the way that the official organizations in Scandinavia practice Ásatrú that supports the Folkish ideas. Your blood has nothing to do with your spirituality.

Do You Have to Have Scandinavian Roots or Be White to Be Ásatrú?

No!

Many American heathens descend from Scandinavians and northern Europeans—at least to an extent. Many of them have also taken DNA tests to learn about their ancestry, and their background is a point of pride. This is understandable. Modern life in North America has become very detached from many of the things we need as human beings in order to formulate an identity for ourselves. Looking at where we came from, the origins of our families, is a way to help us get back to the things that seem important to navigate modern life. However, do not get carried away—there is no inherent value in descending from Scandinavians. Your DNA and genes do not come with *something extra* just because there was a Norwegian or Swede or Icelander or Dane involved in your past.

You do not have to be white; you do not have to have any physical connection to Scandinavia to enjoy our stories, appreciate our ancient philosophy, or worship our gods. Tradition is part of the intangible world heritage. If it calls to you, follow the path!

Is Ásatrú the Same as Wicca?

As I have mentioned earlier in this book, Ásatrú and Wicca did for some time follow the same tracks, as the early thinkers in the 20th century were learning about the ancient traditions as best they could at the time. In modern days, however, Ásatrú has very much found its own way and only in vague terms relates to Wicca. There are Wiccans who practice a branch of northern Wicca, which seems very similar to Ásatrú, but it is not the same.

Is Ásatrú Related to Satanism?

Are there any similarities between Ásatrú and Satanism? Since Christianity has a long tradition of equating heathen practices with the devil, there are some confusing overlaps. However, in essence, there is nothing about Ásatrú that has anything to do with Satanism. Heathens see the ideas of heaven and hell as fictions that have little to do with living life on Earth as it is now. Heathen gods are not controlled by Satan and they have nothing to do with fantasies of scary demons and what you may see in horror movies. Ásatrú has more in common with Hinduism in India, Shinto in Japan, Yoruba in West Africa, and Native American religions in North America than it does with the mythology of Christianity.

Do You Have to Sacrifice Animals to Be Heathen?

No. You do not have to sacrifice anything, offer anything, or do anything at all to identify as heathen. You can be heathen and Ásatrú exactly in the way you wish to be.

Are Modern Heathens Not Just Reenactors?

No—modern heathens do not necessarily dress up in Viking Age garments. It is true that there are some heathens who like to do so, but it does not have much to do with their spiritual ideas. Similarly, there are plenty of reenactors who simply do it as a hobby and have no religious or spiritual connection to the Viking Age. You do not have to wear Viking Age clothes—or even own anything that has to do with the Viking Age—to be a heathen.

Are Modern Heathens Actually Serious about Their Spirituality?

For some people it can be difficult to understand why someone would want to revive an ancient spirituality like heathenism, but heathens are very serious about it. It is a meaningful worldview for many people nowadays, and heathenism fulfills a role that other religions and spiritualities cannot.

Do Heathens Have Moral Values?

The idea that heathens are depraved individuals is based mainly in prejudice and ancient propaganda. Certainly, there are people who come to heathenism and Ásatrú because they see it as a free space for defining their own moral values, but there is, and has always been, a firm moral basis for being heathen. In this book, I have described many of the tenets of the moral basis as it appears in *Hávamál*. Heathens, however, do not really focus on the same things, in terms of moral values, as religions such as Christianity.

ÁSATRÚ IN EUROPE

In Europe, Ásatrú and other spiritualities that have their origin in native pre-Christian cultures have grown exponentially over the years. There are Ásatrú groups in every European country, with a few exceptions, and the heathen movements are growing steadily. Along with Ásatrú, the old Roman religion Religio Romana, the Greek Hellenismos, the Lithuanian Romuva, Iberian folk-religion in Spain, Slavic folk-religion in eastern Europe, Celtic traditions and Anglo-Saxon religion in the British Isles, and Sámi tradition in northern Scandinavia are becoming more and more noticeable. The 21st century is certainly a period for revival of ancient spiritualities across the world. Local native traditions that have much in common with Ásatrú are coming back all over the globe.

PRACTICING ÁSATRÚ TODAY

If you wish to practice Ásatrú, this is my advice to you:

> Get a good copy of the Poetic *Edda* and the Prose *Edda*.
> Get a good copy of a compilation of the Sagas of Icelanders.
> Begin experimenting with the way that you would like to connect with the gods and spirits yourself before you seek out a group. Groups can be very rewarding, but it is important to create your independent foundation for how you relate to *your* gods before you open up to outside influence.

> The best groups are always those that are based on friendship more than anything else. Real and honest friendships drive a good group of heathens much further than hierarchies and ideas of true faith.
> Always follow Óðinn's advice in the *Hávamál*. It will be hard to go wrong when you keep that advice in mind. They are the cumulation of hard-earned lessons through countless years, decades, and centuries.
> Always follow your heart. It is that simple.

WALKING THE PATH OF THE NORTHERN WAY

What brings people to Ásatrú and heathenism, and how do you walk the path of the northern way in the hustle and bustle of modern life?

As human beings we all need to feel grounded, and we all need to feel that our lives are connected to a meaningful community. Many aspects of modern life have left us longing for a community and a sense of direction. Many feel a disconnect from nature, and from those experiences of being present—right here in the now—that our grandparents or ancestors had. Children today may grow up with less birdsong in their lives. They can grow up without ever seeing a common butterfly or a bumblebee. In this modern world, we are quickly losing touch with the community of the world around us, the nature that used to be in our backyard. It is an ironic circumstance of being part of an ever more connected humanity—a humanity that connects us through technology, not community.

The search for a more substantial meaning in a world where technology is taking over and cityscapes are becoming the reality for more and more people brings many to the revival of ancient pre-Christian and pre-Islamic traditions. In some ways, these traditions have the capacity to teach us how to reconnect with nature: to reconnect with the ocean, the mountains, the streams, the weeds, the trees, the fields, the sky, the sun—all the things in this world that, if you pause for a second and look up, remind you of their importance and the fact that you could not exist without them. It is the awareness that our ancient ancestors, whomever they were, once communicated with a world full of animals, plants, fish, birds—and *life*—that brings us to these ancient traditions. We know that if we can just tune in—if we can just understand that old language that was lost with the conversions, with industrialization, and with modernity—then we have the chance for a better future.

Walking the path of the northern way, as an Ásatrúar, a heathen, is very much a matter of choosing to listen to the world around you. It is a matter of becoming conscious about the world outside the domain of the daily grind. It is all about finding a little time in your life to stop and breathe and look back to all those people who came before us, all the ancestors and all their hard work that brought us where we are now, and celebrating their efforts. Our ancestors, regardless of where they came from and what they believed in, carried with them the core of the heathen ethos: *Celebrate life*.

By speaking of this celebration of life in terms of the heathen ways, as Óðinn's wisdom or Freyja's love; by taking a pause in the fast-paced modern life in the form of a blót ritual, rune-reading, or seiðr-working, modern heathens are reconnecting to an ancient, deep wisdom that we are close to forgetting today.

GLOSSARY

PRONUNCIATION KEY FOR NORSE LANGUAGE:

A is usually open: "ah" or like the a in "far."
E is pronounced as an English a: "a" like "late."
I is pronounced like ee in English: "ee" like "leek."
O is pronounced like oa in English: "oa" like "oath."
U is pronounced like oo in English: "oo" like in "look."
Ei is pronounced like a in "lame" or ay in "hay."
Au does not have an equivalent sound in English but sounds a little like u in "hurl" or i in "girl."

Æsir: Gods.

Álf: Spirit.

Álfablót: Winter celebration.

Álfar: Spirits.

Allsherjargoði: High priest.

Ásatrú: Belief in the *æsir*.

Ásatrúar: Believer in the *æsir*.

Áss: God.

Ástvinr: Loving friend of a god/A god is your loving friend.

Ásynja: Goddess.

Ásynjur: Goddesses.

Berserkir: Bear-warriors.

Blót: Ritual, sacrifice, offering.

Bönd: The bonds, the gods.

Dís: Goddess.

Dísir: Goddesses.

Dísþing: Assembly of the *dísir*, spring celebration.

Draugar: Ghosts.

Dvergar: Demons.

Dvergr: Demon.

Edda: Grandmother. The title of Snorri Sturluson's work on Norse mythology from 1220 CE, and the word used for ancient Scandinavian poetry.

Ellepike: Tree spirit.

Erilaz: Earl, jarl.

Fjölkynngi: Magic.

Forn siðr: Ancient custom, tradition.

Fulltrúi: Encompassing dedication to one god.

Fylgja: Spirit animal, dream animal.

Gæfu: The personal abilities that you create.

Galdr: Song magic.

Gandr: Staff magic.

Gardvord: House god.

Gipta: That which has been given to you from birth.

Goðar: Male heathen priests.

Goði: Male heathen priest.

Gói: First month of spring.

Gyðja: Female heathen priest.

Gyðjur: Female heathen priests.

Hammingja: The way you carry yourself.

Hamr: Body-shroud.

Haustr: Fall celebration.

Hávamál: *The Speech of High*. The poem in which Óðinn gives advice on behavior and moral values.

Havfolk: Sea spirits, drowned sailors.

Heathen: A person of the Germanic commons, a practitioner of the old tradition.

Hof: Temple.

Höpt: Those who bind, the gods.

Hugr: Mind, personal spirit.

Huldra: Local spirit.

Huldur: Local spirits.

Innangarðs: Inside the enclosure.

Îrminsûl: The world pillar, represents the world tree.

Jól: Winter celebration.

Jólablót: Winter celebration (ritual).

Jötnar: Demons, ogres.

Jötunn: Demon, ogre.

Julebukk: Yule goat.

Knésetja: Naming ceremony.

Midsommarstång: Midsummer Pole.

Miðsumarr: Midsummer celebration.

Níðstöng: Banning pole, shaming pole.

Nisse: House god.

Nøkken: Spirit of lakes and streams.

Nornagraut: The porridge that is shared with the *nornir* after giving birth.

Nornaspor: The mark of the *nornir*.

Nornir: Goddesses of fate.

Öndvégissúlur: Pillars of the spirit-way, totem pillars.

Ørlög: Ancient law, the fate of the world and each human.

Ôstarûn: The southern German spring celebration.

Ragnarøk: The reign of the gods.

Ragnarökk: The darkness of the gods.

Regin: The Powers.

Sælfolk: Seal spirits/people.

Seiðr: Shamanic magic.

Sigrblót: Spring/Summer celebration.

Skogsrå: Forest demon.

Stallr: Altar, pedestal.

Troll: Demon, ogre.

Tröll: Demons, ogres.

Trolldom: Magic.

Þing: Assembly.

Þióð: Tribe, people, nation.

Þórshelgi: Celebration of the six Thursdays before winter solstice.

Þulr: Heathen priest.

Þurs: Demon, ogre.

Þursar: Demons, ogres.

Úlfheðnar: Wolf-warriors.

Urðarbrunnr: The well of Urðr, fate.

Útangarðs: Outside the enclosure.

Útiseta: Sitting outside, magic, shamanism, meditation.

Vætti: Spirit.

Vættir: Spirits.

Van: God.

Vanir: Gods.

Väntljusstaken: The candleholder for the waiting candles during *Þórshelgi*.

Vár: Spring.

Varðlokkur: Shamanic singing.

Vé: Holy site.

Vébönd: The ropes or bonds that mark a holy site.

Vetrnætur: Fall/Winter celebration.

Völuspá: *The Prophecy of the Völva*. The prophetic Eddic poem that tells of the creation and destruction of the world.

Vølva: Heathen priestess.

Wyrd's Web: Fate.

Yggdrasill: The world tree.

RESOURCES

Books

The Complete Sagas of Icelanders, including 49 tales. Edited by Viðarr Hreinsson. Reykjavík: Leifur Eiríksson Publishing. 1997.

A Dictionary of Northern Mythology. Rudolf Simek. Suffolk: D. S. Brewer. 2008.

Edda. Snorri Sturluson. Translated by Anthony Faulkes. Dent: Everyman's Library. 1995.

Heimskringla: The History of the Norwegian Kings. Translated by Lee M. Hollander. Austin: University of Austin Texas. 1995.

Norse Mythology. Neil Gaiman. New York: W. W. Norton & Company. 2017.

The Norse Myths: A Guide to Gods and Heroes. Carolyne Larrington. London: Thames & Hudson. 2017.

The Poetic Edda. Translated by Carolyne Larrington. Oxford: Oxford's World Classics. 2009.

The Sagas of the Icelanders. Edited by Jane Smiley. London: Penguin. 2005.

Saxo Grammaticus: History of the Danes. Translated by Peter Fischer. Suffolk: D.S. Brewer. 1979.

Online Resources

The Troth is an Ásatrú group in the United States: TheTroth.org

Asatru UK is a group for Ásatrú in the United Kingdom: AsatruUK.org

A great place to connect with Ásatrúar and heathens online is the Facebook group *Huginn's Heathen Hof*.

A great page for information on Ásatrú and heathenism is Mimisbrunnr.info by Joseph Hopkins.

REFERENCES

Primary Sources

Danmarks Folkesagn 1–2. Edited by Just Mathias Thiele. Copenhagen, 1843.

Edda. Die Lieder des Codex Regius nebst verwandten Denkmälern. Edited by Gustav Neckel and Hans Kuhn. Heidelberg: Carl Winter Universitätsverlag, 1962.

Germania. P. Cornelius Tacitus. Edited by Richard Hünnerkopf. Translated by Eugen Fehrle, 5th edition. Heidelberg: Carl Winter Universitätsverlag, 1959.

Gesta Hammaburgensis ecclesiae pontificum: Scriptores Rerum Germanicarum in usum scholarum ex monumentis germaniae historicis separatim editi. Magistri Adam Bremensis. Edited by Bernhard Schmiedler, 3rd edition. Leipzig: Hahnsche Buchhandlung, 1917.

Gesta Normannorum seu de moribus et actis primorum Normanniae ducum. Edited by Felice Lifshitz. Berlin: Fécamp, 1996.

Ibn Fadlan, Ahmad. *Mission to the Volga.* Translation by J. E. Montgomery. New York: NYU Press. 2017.

Íslenzk Fornrit I–XXXIII. Edited by various. Reykjavík: Hið Íslenska Fornritafélag, 1930–2018.

Saxo Grammaticus: Gesta Danorum, 1–2. Edited by Karsten Friis-Jensen. Translated by Peter Zeeberg. Copenhagen: Det Danske Sprog- og Litteratur-selskab and Gads Forlag, 2005.

Snorri Sturluson. *Edda. Háttatal.* Edited by Anthony Faulkes. Oxford: Clarendon Press, 1991.

Snorri Sturluson. *Edda. Prologue and Gylfaginning.* Edited by Anthony Faulkes. Oxford: Clarendon Press, 1982.

Snorri Sturluson. *Edda. Skáldskaparmál.* Edited by Anthony Faulkes. London: Viking Society for Northern Research, 1998.

Secondary Sources

Alver, Bente G. "Concepts of the Soul in Norwegian Tradition." In *Nordic Folklore: Recent Studies*, edited by Reimund Kvideland and Henning K. Sehmsdorf in collaboration with Elizabeth Simpson, 110–28. Bloomington: Indiana University Press, 1990.

Arntz, Helmut: *Handbuch der Runenkunde.* Halle: Max Niemeier Verlag, 1944.

Baetke, Walter. "Die Götterlehre der Snorra-Edda." In *Walter Baetke. Kleine Schriften. Geschichte, Recht und Religion in germanischem Schrifttum*, edited by Kurt Rudolph and Ernst Walter, 206–46. Weimar: Hermann Böhlaus Nachfolger, 1950. Reprint 1973.

Barnes, Michael. *Runes: A Handbook.* Woodbridge: Boydell, 2012.

Beck, Heinrich. "Die Religionsgeschichtlichen Quellen der Gylfaginning." In *Germanische Religionsgeschichte. Quellen und Quelleprobleme. Reallexikon der germanischen Altertumskund. Ergänzungsbände 5*, edited by Heinrich Beck, Detlev Ellmers, and Kurt Schier, 608–17. Berlin: Walter de Gruyter, 1992.

Brink, Stefan, and Neil Price (eds.). *The Viking World.* London: Routledge, 2012.

Bø, Olav, Ronald Grambo, Bjarne Hodne, and Ørnulf Hodne. *Norske Segner.* Oslo: Samlaget, 1995.

Clunies Ross, Margaret. "The Mythological Fictions of *Snorra Edda*." In *Snorrastefna*, edited by Úlfar Bragason, 204–16. Reykjavík: Stofnun Sigurðar Nordals, 1992.

Clunies Ross, Margaret. "Þórr's Honour." In *Studien zum Altgermanischen. Festschrift für Heinrich Beck*, edited by Heiko Uecker, 48–76. Berlin: Walter de Gruyter, 1994.

Clunies Ross, Margaret. *Prolonged Echoes. Volume 1.* Odense: Odense Universitetsforlag, 1994.

Clunies Ross, Margaret. *Prolonged Echoes. Volume 2.* Odense: Odense Universitetsforlag, 1998.

Clunies Ross, Margaret. *Skáldskaparmál: Snorri Sturluson's Ars Poetica and Medieval Theories of Language.* Odense: Odense Universitetsforlag, 1987.

Clunies Ross, Margaret. "Snorri Sturluson's use of the Norse origin-legend of the sons of Fornjótr in his Edda." *Arkiv för nordisk filologi* 98 (1983): 47–66.

Clunies Ross, Margaret. "Two Old Icelandic Theories of Ritual." In *Old Norse Myths, Literature and Society,* edited by Margaret Clunies Ross, 279–99. Odense: University Press of Southern Denmark, 2003.

Davidson, Hilda R. E. *Gods and Myths of Northern Europe.* Harmondsworth: Penguin Books, 1964.

De Vries, Jan. *Altgermanische Religionsgeschichte,* vols. 1–2. Berlin: De Gruyter, 1970.

Dronke, Ursula. "Classical Influences on Early Norse Literature." In *Classical Influences on European Culture A.D. 500–1500. Proceedings of an International Conference held at King's College, Cambridge, April 1969,* edited by R. R. Bolgar, 143–50. London: Cambridge University Press, 1971.

Dronke, Ursula. *The Poetic Edda. Volume 2. Mythological Poems.* Oxford: Clarendon Press, 1997.

Dronke, Ursula. "The War of the Æsir and Vanir." In *Idee. Gestalt. Geschichte. Festschrift Klaus von See. Studien zur europäischen Kulturtradition,* edited by G. W. Weber, 223–38. Odense: Odense University Press, 1988.

Dronke, Ursula, and Peter Dronke. "The Prologue of the Prose Edda: Explorations of a Latin Background." In *Sjötiu Ritgerðir: Festskrift til Jakob Benediktsson,* edited by Einar G. Pétursson and Jónas Kristjánsson, 153–76. Reykjavík, 1977.

DuBois, Thomas. *Nordic Religions in the Viking Age*. Philadelphia: University of Pennsylvania Press, 1999.

Dumézil, George. *Le festin d'immortalité: Étude de mythologie comparée indo-européenne*. Paris: Librairie Orientaliste Paul Geuthner, 1924.

Dumézil, George. *Les dieux des Germains: Essai sur la formation de le religion scandinave*. Paris: Presses Universitaires de France, 1959.

Faulkes, Anthony. "Pagan Sympathy: Attitudes to Heathendom in the Prologue to Snorra Edda." In *Edda: A Collection of Essays*, edited by Robert J. Glendinning and Haraldur Bessason, 283–314. Canada: University of Manitoba Press, 1983.

Flowers, Stephen. *Icelandic Magic: Practice Secrets of the Northern Grimoires*. Rochester: Inner Traditions, 2016.

Gardell, Mattias. *Gods of the Blood: The Pagan Revival and White Separatism*. Durham: Duke University Press, 2003.

Grimm, Jacob. *Deutsche Mythologie, 1–2*. Göttingen: Dieterichsche Buchhandlung, 1854.

Gunnell, Terry. "Eddic Poetry." *Old Norse-Icelandic Literature and Culture*, edited by Rory McTurk, 82–100. Oxford: Blackwell Publishing, 2007.

Hastrup, Kirsten. "Cosmology and Society in Medieval Iceland." *Ethnologia Scandinavica* 11 (1981): 63–78.

Hastrup, Kirsten. *Culture and History in Medieval Iceland*. Oxford: Clarendon Press, 1985.

Hastrup, Kirsten. *Island of Anthropology*. Odense: Odense University Press, 1990.

Jesch, Judith. "Memorials in Speech and Writing." In *Hikuin 32*, 95–104. Moesgård: Forlaget Hikuin, 2005.

Kristjánsson, Jónas. *Eddas and Sagas: Iceland's Medieval Literature*. Translation by Peter Foote. Reykjavík: Hið íslenska bókmenntafélag, 2007.

Larrington, Carolyne. *The Norse Myths: A Guide to Gods and Heroes*. London: Thames & Hudson, 2017.

Lindow, John. *Trolls: An Unnatural History*. London: Reaktion Books, 2014.

Lindow, John. "Bloodfeud and Scandinavian mythology." *Alvissmal* 4 (1994): 51–68.

Lindow, John. "Cultures in Contact." In *Old Norse Myths, Literature and Society*, edited by Margaret Clunies Ross, 89–109. Odense: University Press of Southern Denmark, 2003.

Lindow, John. *Murder and Vengeance Among the Gods*. Helsinki: Suomalainen tiedeakatemia, Academia Scientiarum Fennica, 1997.

Lindow, John. "Íslendingabók and Myth." *Scandinavian Studies* 69 (1997): 455–64.

Lindow, John. "Supernatural Others and Ethnic Others: A Millenium of World View." *Scandinavian Studies* 67 (1995): 8–31.

McKinnell, John. *Both One and Many. Essays on Change and Variety in Late Norse Heathenism*. Rome: "Il Calamo," 1994.

McKinnell, John. "*Hávamál* B: A Poem of Sexual Intrigue." *Saga-Book* 29 (2005): 83–114.

McKinnell, John. *Meeting the Other in Old Norse Myth and Legend*. Cambridge: D. S. Brewer, 2005.

McKinnell, John. "*Vǫluspá* and the Feast of Easter." *Alvíssmál* 12 (2008): 3–28.

McKinnell, John, and Rudolf Simek, with Klaus Düwel. *Runes, Magic and Religion: A Sourcebook*. Wien: Fassbaender, 2004.

Meulengracht Sørensen, Preben. *Fortælling og ære*. Aarhus: Aarhus University Press, 1993.

Mitchell, Stephen A. *Witchcraft and Magic in the Nordic Middle Ages*. Philadelphia: University of Pennsylvania Press, 2011.

Mogk, Eugen. "Novellistische Darstellung mythologischer Stoffe Snorris und seiner Schule." In *FF Communications*, edited by C. W. von Sydow, 3–33. Helsinki: Suomalainen tiedeakatemia, 1923.

Nordberg, Andreas. *Jul, disting och förkyrklig tideräkning. Kalendrar och kalendariska riter i det förkristna Norden*. Uppsala: Kungl. Gustav Adolfs Akademien för svensk folkkultur, 2006.

North, Richard. *Heathen Gods in Old English Literature*. Cambridge: Cambridge University Press, 1997.

Rudgley, Richard: *The Return of Odin: The Modern Renaissance of Pagan Imagination*. Rochester: Inner Traditions, 2006.

Schjødt, Jens Peter. "Diversity and its consequences for the study of Old Norse religion. What is it we are trying to reconstruct?" In *Between Paganism and Christianity in the North*, edited by Leszek P. Słupecki and Jakub Morawiec, 9–22. Rzeszów: Wydawnictwo Uniwersytetu Rzeszowskiego, 2009.

Schjødt, Jens Peter. "Hvad er det i grunden, vi rekonstruerer?" *Religionsvidenskabeligt Tidsskrift* 50 (2007): 33–45.

Schjødt, Jens Peter. *Initiation between Two Worlds. Structure and Symbolism in Pre-Christian Scandinavian Religion*. Odense: Odense University Press, 2008.

Schjødt, Jens Peter. "Myths as Sources for Rituals – Theoretical and Practical Implications." In *Old Norse Myths, Literature and Society*, edited by Margaret Clunies Ross, 261–78. Odense: University of Southern Denmark Press, 2003.

Schjødt, Jens Peter. "Reflections on Aims and Methods in the Study of Old Norse Religion." In *More than Mythology: Narratives, Ritual Practices and Regional Distribution in Pre-Christian Scandinavian Religions*, edited by Catharina Raudvere and Jens Peter Schjødt, 263–87. Lund: Nordic Academic Press, 2011.

Schjødt, Jens Peter. "Teksten mellem kilde og litteratur." In *Den norröna renässansen*, edited by Karl G. Johansson, 179–94. Reykholt: Snorrastofa Cultural and Medieval Centre, 2007.

Sigurðsson, Gísli. *The Medieval Icelandic Saga and Oral Tradition.* Cambridge: The Milman Parry Collection of Oral Literature, Harvard University. Harvard University Press, 2004.

Simek, Rudolph. *Dictionary of Northern Mythology.* Cambridge: Brewer, 2007.

Snook, Jennifer. *American Heathens: The Politics of Identity in a Pagan Religious Movement.* Philadelphia: Temple University Press, 2015.

Steinsland, Gro. *Det hellige bryllup i norrøn kongeideologi. En analyse av hierogami-myten i Skírnismál, Ynglingatal, Háleygjatal og Hyndluljóð.* Larvik: Solum, 1991.

Ström, Folke. *Diser, nornor, valkyrjor. Fruktbarhetskult och sakralt kungadöme i Norden.* Stockholm: Kungliga Vitterhets Historie och Antikvitets Akademiens Handlingar, 1954.

Thorsson, Edred. *Futhark: A Handbook of Rune Magic.* San Francisco: Weiser Books, 1984.

Thorsson, Edred. *Runecaster's Handbook.* San Francisco: Weiser Books, 1999.

Turville-Petre, E. O. G. *Myth and Religion of the North.* London: Weidenfeld and Nicolson, 1964.

Von Schnurbein, Stefanie. *Norse Revival: Transformations of Germanic Neopaganism.* Leiden: Brill, 2016.

Von See, Klaus. *Mythos und Theologie im skandinavischen Hochmittelalter.* Heidelberg: Carl Winter Universitätsverlag, 1988.

Zoëga, Geir T. *A Concise Dictionary of Old Icelandic.* Toronto: University of Toronto Press, 2004.

INDEX

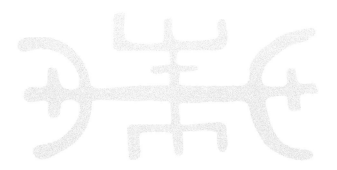

ABOUT THE AUTHOR

 **DR. MATHIAS NORDVIG** has a PhD in Nordic mythology from Aarhus University in Denmark, his native country. He has been teaching Viking studies, Norse mythology, Scandinavian folklore, and Arctic culture at the University of Colorado at Boulder since 2015. He runs a YouTube channel called The Nordic Mythology Channel along with its corresponding website, NordicMythologyChannel.com. He also has a podcast with Daniel Farrand, the co-owner of the clothing company Horns of Odin, called The Nordic Mythology Podcast. In addition to publishing both research and popular fiction about Nordic mythology, Dr. Nordvig works with musicians and visual artists to create inspiring music and art about the Viking Age and Norse mythology. Most recently, Dr. Nordvig has published the book *Norse Mythology for Kids*, a retelling of Norse mythology for children ages 8 to 12.

Printed in the USA
CPSIA information can be obtained
at www.ICGtesting.com
CBHW040308050324
4972CB00013B/108